KEEPING YOUR CROWN

The Black Woman's Guide to Reclaiming Greatness

JOYCE & DEBRA GLENN

Copyright © 2017 by Joyce and Debra Glenn

Cover Design: Joyce and Debra Glenn
Cover Photo: Anthony Thomas
Interior Design: Joyce and Debra Glenn

All rights reserved. No part of this book shall be reproduced by any mechanical, photographic, or electronic process, or in the form of a phonographic recording; nor may it be stored in a retrieval system, transmitted, or otherwise be copied for public or private use—other than for "fair use" as brief quotations embodied in articles and reviews—without prior written permission of the publisher.

This publication contains the opinions and ideas of its author. It is intended to provide helpful and informative material on the subject matter covered. Neither the author nor publisher assumes responsibility for the use or misuse of information contained in this book. The intent of the author is only to offer information of a general nature to help you in your quest for emotional well-being. In the event you use any of the information in this book for yourself, the author and the publisher assume no responsibility for your actions.

Library of Congress Cataloging-in-Publication Data

Glenn, Joyce and Debra.

Keeping Your Crown / Joyce and Debra Glenn.

ISBN 978-1-5410-3987-2

1st edition, January 2017

Printed in the United States of America

CONTENTS

DEDICATION v

PREFACE vii

INTRODUCTION xx

SECTION ONE:

MANAGING OUR LOVE LIVES

Be Harshly Selective With Your Loyalty ……….. 2

Know Exactly Who You Are and
What You Want ………………………………… 6

Don't Lose Yourself in a Relationship …………. 11

Be Open-Minded …………………………….. 18

Be Nice ………………………………………. 21

SECTION TWO:

UNDERSTANDING MEN

Women are to be Loved, Men are
to be Understood 31

Understanding a Man's Purpose 34

Let Men Pursue You 37

Don't Let men Dictate the Way You
Feel About the Way You Look ……................... 42

SECTION THREE:

MANAGING HOW WE TREAT EACH OTHER

What Type of Woman Are You? 53

How to Handle Your Thoughts
and Judgements 65

How to Handle Judgement When
You're on the Receiving End 66

SECTION FOUR:

CHANGING OUR VIEWS ON SINGLE MOTHERHOOD

How Single Motherhood is Perceived 76

The Effects on Your Child 94

How "Daddy Issues" are Destroying
"Black Love" 114

Remember, Your Child Is Not Your Friend 118

How Your Decision to Date
Affects Your Child 124

The Single Exception to
Single Motherhood 127

Oops! I'm a Baby Momma…What Now? 148

SECTION FIVE:

MANAGING OUR SELF-IMAGE

Be Educated 168

Be Selfish 171

Be Healthy 187

Be Cultured 204

CONCLUSION 211

ABOUT THE AUTHORS 217

DEDICATION

DEDICATION

We want to dedicate this book to our father, 1SG Charlie Mac Glenn. You are truly the best father, role model and friend anyone could ever dream of having. You were always supportive of our dreams and encouraged us to believe in ourselves and pursue our passions, no matter how challenging or unattainable they seemed. We thank you for the outstanding example you provided by demonstrating hard work, discipline, structure and character all while maintaining a light-hearted disposition and a true zest for life. We appreciate all the sacrifices you made for our family and we have never taken them for granted. You are a true example of a father, a soldier, a king and an honorable man. You will forever be missed. We love you and may you rest in paradise. Hooah! We would also like to dedicate this book to our mother, Matilda, the matriarch of our family and a true example of a queen. You give to no end and without you; we have absolutely no idea how our

DEDICATION

family would function! You are the reason we understand the amount of sacrifice required to be an outstanding wife, mother and woman. We strive to be half the woman you are considering your strength, intellect, dignity, wisdom and compassion seem almost impossible to match! You have fulfilled the role as a mother figure to so many people outside of your own children. Your Sunday dinners have feed countless mouths and have served as a source of comfort and joy for so many. You are a godsend and we hope to one day make you as proud as you have made us. This book is also dedicated to our sisters who are the motivation for our hard work and to our nieces and nephew, who are the reasons we want to leave this world better than we found it.

PREFACE

As with many conscious black people, we have always had an intense desire to see the black community arrive at a place that is thriving and prosperous. It would be gratifying to witness our community eradicate the psychological dysfunctions created by the institution of slavery. After enduring white America's countless attempts to strip us of our human dignity, we deserve a functioning and respectable existence considering it was our free labor that established this country's economic dominance. We literally built the foundation on which this country rests, yet we are corruptly denied equal opportunities. It is demoralizing that black Americans are still subjected to discrimination and civil injustices. However, without a unified plan and a sense of comradery, these circumstances will not change. There are modifications black people can implement to accelerate progress, like changing our mindset and our behaviors. The black community needs mending on

PREFACE

many levels, however this book specifically addresses black women and what we can do to advance Black America. This book focuses on how black women can improve their life choices to make a positive impact within the black community.

Black women are unaware to what extent their decisions can either advance the state of Black America or contribute to its demise. The black woman's role in inspiring change is monumental. So, for black women to continue to make life choices without understanding and acknowledging the magnitude of their influence can be disastrous. This book reminds black women of their responsibilities and reinforces how crucial it is that we act with purpose and intention to improve our circumstances. This book specifically discusses how to structure our love lives, how to strengthen our sisterhood, how to build strong families and how to improve our self-image in ways that will advance our communities. This book encourages black women to redefine "what is normal" and will challenge them to stop becoming "baby mommas." Black women must reevaluate how we view single motherhood because there is no future for Black America if our children do not

PREFACE

have dedicated fathers within a stable, two-parent nuclear family. This book will challenge black women to think and behave in ways that are reflective our true greatness to advance the state of Black America.

People may be wondering what inspired us to write a book challenging black women to aspire to achieve greatness to advance the state of the black community. They may be curious as to how actresses, models and "video vixens" would even be concerned, let alone, passionately interested. We attribute these interests and passions to our parents as well as to a few extraordinary black women (who we'll mention later) who inspired us throughout our journey. Their lessons molded the ideals that have kept us focused and head-smart while navigating college, the entertainment industry and our lives in general. Their impact on our lives reinforces the notion that a solid family foundation and positive role models are vital parts of success.

We can attest to the power of intentional parenting and how it can determine a child's mindset and level of success. Our dad was born in a shack in Sledge, Mississippi and our mother also grew up in humble beginnings in Marks, Mississippi. As teenagers, for part-time work, they

PREFACE

chopped cotton for seven dollars a day during the brutally hot summers for spending money. They were no strangers to hard work and sacrifice and they constantly stressed the importance of "taking every generation up a notch." Our parents insisted, when starting a family, the goal should be to provide your children with a better life experience than your own. Our parents were intentional in ensuring our lives were much better than theirs. Needless to say, they achieved this. At age 18, our father enlisted in the U.S. Army to broaden his opportunities. He understood he could not obtain the life he envisioned for himself or his future family by remaining in Mississippi. Our father was right for following his instincts and joining the armed forces because it afforded us an upbringing we thoroughly enjoyed. We felt blessed as children, traveling the world, experiencing new cultures and taking advantage of the amazing education system the military lifestyle provided. By joining the armed forces, our father was also able to take advantage of the GI Bill, allowing him to obtain a college degree. Our mother was also a first generation college graduate. So, in addition to insisting that a person must take their family up a generation, our parents demonstrated that education is the

PREFACE

ultimate equalizer, allowing the upward mobility needed to transcend your socioeconomic status. Besides providing a life that was far removed from their upbringing, the day-to-day lectures and lessons our parents instilled in us made us the women we are today.

Through her behavior, choices, and capabilities our mother demonstrated how to be a strong and dignified woman. Growing up, our mother had an exceptionally close relationship with her great-grandmother. Her great-grandmother was born in 1882, less than 20 years after slavery ended so, our mother's great-great-grandmother was actually a slave. When raising us and our two older sisters, our mother often passed down lessons told by her great-grandmother. One message she often reinforced was that we, African Americans, are the descendants of the strongest black men and women in this country. Millions of men, women and children did not survive the unimaginable conditions that existed during the transatlantic slave trade. So although our history is one associated with unthinkable injustice, violence, hatred and greed imposed upon us by white America, it does not negate the fact that we survived! We are the descendants of men and women who are resilient

PREFACE

and unbreakable! As our mother passed this message onto us, it served as a reminder that as strong black women, our capabilities are limitless.

In addition to encouraging us to take pride in our heritage, instead of using typical terms of endearment, our mother often referred to us as her black Nubian princesses. We are uncertain, that at age five or six, we could conceptualize what that meant but as adults we can attest that she was instilling self-love, pride and self-acceptance. As a result, even if black women were underrepresented or poorly represented in society or in the media, it never had a negative impact on how we felt about ourselves as black women. Our mother truly invested in our self-esteem and was intentional in raising children with a healthy self-image. We learned that if these values are instilled in the home, young girls will understand and believe in the power and strength they possess as black queens and will manage their lives accordingly. Now as adults, we understand our responsibility to convey this message to black women who may be unaware of their worth.

Aside from statistics and studies, we can attest to the monumental impact a father has on his children's safety and

PREFACE

self-esteem. In addition to protecting and providing for our family, our father made a conscious effort to raise his daughters to become intelligent and respectable women. One principle our dad advocated was the idea that a woman should never solely rely on her looks to succeed and should instead nurture her intellect and work ethic to excel. For instance, if we ever spent too much time in the mirror getting ready, he would say "work on the inside more than the outside." He was planting the seeds necessary to prevent his daughters from becoming bimbos. He was constantly reinforcing the importance of having more to offer than superficial qualities. Needless to say, this greatly motivated our notable academic success throughout both high school and college. In addition to the typical obstacles young girls must overcome, working in the entertainment industry introduced a unique set of challenges. The temptations and distractions of this industry can easily alter the course of a young woman's life. Having the support of involved parents and the influence of positive role models, made it possible for us to navigate such an enticing industry. While working in entertainment, we were often commended on our poise and the level of respect we commanded while

PREFACE

working in a male dominated industry. Honestly, we cannot take responsibility for this. It is greatly attributable to our parents and especially our father's presence and influence. As a matter of fact, our father took us to our first music video audition. Prior to doing music videos, we had been modeling under agency representation. Our parents were supportive of our careers to the extent that it did not interfere with our education. They always emphasized the importance of education but they also encouraged us to follow our dreams and pursue our passions. So, when modeling agents began casting models for big budget music videos, our father accompanied us to our first booking. In fact, we were only 17 years old on our first music video set, so our father insisted on being present. We didn't understand at the time but he was setting a tone and building a reputation for us. He wanted to make it clear that we were not to be mistreated without reprimand. Again, this reinforced our understanding of man's purpose in a woman's life—to serve as a protector. He set a precedent that made it easier for us to navigate the industry and make good choices. As one could imagine, the entertainment industry can be an enticing place to work for a young

PREFACE

woman. However, it is also flooded with temptation and negative influences. Having a father who invested in our character and values helped us avoid the mistakes that many women make. We were often approached by powerful men like rappers, other artists and athletes but our relationship with our father allowed us, even at an early age, to decipher whether a man's intentions were sincere. In most cases their intentions were not but our upbringing allowed us to avoid potentially harmful experiences. We know countless women who were used up and exploited by ill-intentioned men. We've witnessed countless young women become damaged and broken because of their inability to survive the temptations of this industry. So, if the influence of an involved father can help women navigate an industry flooded with as many distractions as the entertainment industry, it is evident how vitally important fathers are in steering their daughters down the right path.

When Karrine Steffans recounted many of the horrid events that took place throughout her career, like drug abuse and rape, in her memoir *Confessions of a Video Vixen*, we were well aware of the possibility of these things happening to a young woman. We understand how the "glitz and

PREFACE

glam" surrounding that lifestyle can lure in young women. We also understand that the only difference between the choices we made at such a young age and the choices she made are the result of having support vs. not having support. There are few differences between the well-known "Super Head" and The Glenn Twins, except for our upbringing. Karrine is a beautiful, intelligent and resilient woman; however parental guidance is crucial in influencing one's choices. We are in no way more morally astute than she, we simply had support. So, it is clear how vitally important it is for young women to have a strong support system. In order for our young queens to avoid life's pitfalls and grow into women who can become positive agents of change within the black community, we must place more emphasis on building and sustaining strong black families.

The reality is, strong families breed strong children and strong families are the foundation for strong communities. In order to strengthen the condition of the black community, we must raise our standards for how black families are structured and exert more effort into ensuring they function. Black women have a huge impact on how black families are created and therefore must take

PREFACE

this undertaking seriously. We love being black and we love our black brothers and sisters. If we want our communities to arrive at a place that is thriving and strong enough to overcome what we have been through, it will require immense change, initiative and effort to repair the black family structure.

We are not therapists nor do we proclaim to have their credentials. We are simply entertainers with a high moral compass. Our journey has not been perfect or easy but we firmly believe in carrying life lessons forward. As a result of both our good choices and our mistakes, we accumulated knowledge that can assist women in learning how to love themselves, find happiness and avoid setbacks. In addition to our parents, there are many strong, beautiful and respectable queens that have truly inspired us and the lives of countless black women. As tribute to their accomplishments and influence, we included quotes from Maya Angelou, Oprah Winfrey, Iyanla Vanzant, Michelle Obama and Susan L. Taylor to further reinforce the messages conveyed in this book. These women are remarkable black queens and are true examples of what black women are capable of contributing to the black

PREFACE

community and society as a whole. Like the role models who inspired us, it is our obligation to help other women navigate life's challenges. We understand the importance of sharing the lessons we learned to inspire women to reach their full potential. Empowering women and resolving social issues within the black community is truly our passion. It is our priority to ensure black women understand their worth and in turn raise their standards for themselves, understanding that as queens, their influence is essential to advancing the state of Black America.

INTRODUCTION

INTRODUCTION

It is becoming increasingly obvious that an urgent need for reform within the black community is long overdue. Several recent and not-so-recent incidences taking place in this country reinforce this dire need for change. These incidences are occurring so frequently they leave an implication that blacks are deemed unimportant, ignorable and disposable in the eyes of some groups of people in this country. One of the countless examples was the lack of immediate relief in response to Hurricane Katrina that left tens of thousands of predominately black men, women and children dead or displaced and in a state of crisis. Another example is the mass incarceration of black men that is destroying black families and serves as a modern day form of slavery. One of the most appalling and transparent examples is the constant and senseless murders of countless black people committed by police officers with impunity. It

INTRODUCTION

is a natural response to get angry and a justifiable response to seek retaliation. However, one underutilized but necessary response while on the path to finding resolution is self-examination.

Black people need to take a moment and assess where we are as a people. It is certainly important to continue to confront and protest the injustices constantly being inflicted upon us. But in addition to confronting our oppressors we must also confront ourselves. We must demand more from ourselves as individuals and demand more from our black brothers and sisters. We have to literally treat "us" the way we demand to be treated by others. If the idea of a police officer gunning down an unarmed black man makes us outraged, we have to condition our community to feel the same opposition to the idea of one black man killing another. In addition to advocating causes like Black Lives Matter, we must demonstrate this philosophy within our own communities. We have to develop a sense of unity, respect and protectiveness for each other. The idea that a person shows others how to treat them, according to how they treat themselves, is an ideology that is also applicable for a

INTRODUCTION

collective group of people. Every individual black person must treat themselves and other black people with the respect and dignity we are demanding from others. It is time for Black America to have a harsh and honest self-assessment. We must face the fact that if we do not take ourselves seriously, hold ourselves to higher standards and treat "us" as if we are important and valuable, no one else will. We can't continue to perpetuate violence against each other within our own communities. We can't display a lack of regard for the lives of our brothers and sisters and expect others to value their lives. It is time for black people to work together to rebuild black communities. It is time for black people to redefine "what is normal." We must no longer deem mediocrity, reckless behavior and a lack of discipline tolerable within the black community to ensure that we become a powerful force. There are many changes that need to take place in order for Black America to become reflective of our true greatness and strength. There are also many tactics that can and should be used in our fight for equality. However, one impactful way to remedy many of the problems facing Black America is through one

INTRODUCTION

of the black communities' most valuable resources—black women.

Black women are strong, loyal, dependable, resourceful, dignified and sincere. Black women have the strength, foresight and compassion to not only be respected alongside a man as his partner but are also astute and valuable leaders. When at our best we are supportive and encouraging wives and partners and nurturing and highly respected mothers. All of mankind comes from the womb of a black woman and in turn, the title "queen" innately belongs to the black woman. Black women possess a beauty that is so unique and intriguing, other women go to great lengths to imitate our full lips, our tanned skin, our hairstyles, our shapely figures and even the way we dance. Black women must reacquaint themselves with their beauty and strength, never again allowing our significance or worth to be denied or devalued. We must fulfil our responsibility to be role models in our families and communities.

Many black women are unaware to what extent they can initiate change in the black community. It is time for black women to deliberately use their strength and power to enhance their lives and the condition of the black

INTRODUCTION

community. It is an understatement to say, when at our best, black women are capable of remarkable successes. But we must question our choices and shortcomings because they contradict the ideals we once stood for. We cannot allow our actions and behaviors to be inconsistent with the greatness, power and resilience that is characteristic of our ancestors. We must ask ourselves, "How did we stray so far from where we once were?" It is imperative that we take our role within our community seriously. To become pillars of society, we must evaluate and improve the way we are living our lives. We cannot call ourselves queens while leading lives that make us unworthy of this title. We cannot be great if we make unintelligent choices or lead mediocre lives. We have to raise our personal expectations so that we represent ourselves accurately. Once again, black women must redefine "what is normal" and acceptable behavior. It is time to neglect lazy ideals that imply it is okay to settle for mediocre relationships, that it's acceptable to be uneducated, that it's okay to be unhealthy, that it's okay to have children without the support of a marriage or that it's okay to have children without proper resources. There is an attack on the future of Black America. In order for black

INTRODUCTION

women to uplift and protect the black community, we must conduct ourselves using a higher consciousness. We must understand how vitally important it is to operate at our absolute best in our personal lives and within our communities. It is time for black women to have a heart-to-heart with self and answer these vital questions: What type of woman should I become to be happy with self? What standards should I set for my life that will display pride for my ancestors and my future legacies? How should I conduct myself to ensure that I am a positive agent of change within the black community?

Once black women understand and accept the influence we have in initiating change, we can advance the black community to a place that reflects our best efforts. Black women determine the values that are important to our families and our communities. It is our responsibility to construct a mental image of success for Black America and strive to make life choices consistent with that image. We must live with intention and purpose if we want to reclaim our greatness. To do so, we must change the way we are managing our love lives, change the way we view men,

INTRODUCTION

change the way we treat other black women, change our views on single motherhood, and change our self-image.

SECTION ONE:
MANAGING OUR LOVE LIVES

Be Harshly Selective With Your Loyalty · Know Exactly Who You Are and What You Want · Don't Lose Yourself in a Relationship · Be Open-Minded · Be Nice

1

SECTION ONE:
MANAGING OUR LOVE LIVES

"Be willing to share all of who you are. So many of us want a partner, but we're not willing to show all of us." –
Iyanla Vanzant

Cultivating healthy relationships and strong partnerships are essential to a woman's happiness and wellbeing. Because women invest heavily into romantic relationships, it is important that these interactions are nurturing, positive and productive. In order for black women to remain focused on their purpose, their goals and their growth, they cannot be distracted or stifled by toxic or counterproductive relationships. To build and sustain constructive relationships, we must establish high standards and appropriate expectations from dating. If a woman allows a man or a useless relationship to tear her down, she will be incapable of serving as a positive agent of change within the black community. So, we must ensure that we are harshly selective with our loyalty while dating. We must not allow a relationship to define who we are so we do not lose ourselves in a relationship. We must know exactly what we want and fully understand what we offer in a relationship. We must also be open-minded and respectful while pursuing fulfilling love lives. When we form supportive and uplifting partnerships, we can build strong families which are the foundation for thriving black communities.

BE HARSHLY SELECTIVE WITH YOUR LOYALTY

Among the many amazing qualities black women possess, our loyalty is one of our greatest. However, let's not neglect that, paired with that loyalty is a demanding partner with high expectations. Black women have a reputation for being a bit tough to date. This is simply because we have an innate desire to challenge and motivate men to reach their full potential. As queens we desire to be matched with a king. If a man can rise to the occasion, there is no question that once a black woman decides she loves you, her support and encouragement will stand the test of time. We have all heard and had plenty of good laughs at the witticisms about white women leaving faster than a speeding bullet the second her man undergoes financial hardship. Black women however, possess a kind of strength that allows us to remain dedicated even when life circumstances become difficult or uncomfortable.

The black woman's loyalty undoubtedly deserves acclaim but because providing this type of support is so invaluable, black women must start being incredibly selective with whom they give their loyalty. We must stop being loyal to men who do not protect us, provide for us or improve the quality of our lives. Our ability to provide unconditional devotion is only special when we gift it to the right person. We should never allow ourselves to give more than what is necessary or reasonable, simply because we are strong enough to give it.

KEEPING YOUR CROWN

"You can never love anyone to your own detriment. That is not love, that is possession, control, fear, or a combination of them all." –Iyanla Vanzant

Considering black women are naturally dedicated, it is understandable that a woman would feel accomplished when supporting her man. Some women will go as far as adopting titles like "a ride or die chick," to express their intense dedication. Unfortunately, some women take this gesture too far by giving their loyalty prematurely or by being loyal to an undeserving man. Never "hold a man down" if he doesn't improve your quality of life, ensure your comfortability, respect you and treat you like his queen. You should only give loyalty to a man who is reliable. He should be so dependable you could call him at a moment's notice to change a flat tire and he would be there. If you are startled by a strange noise in the middle of the night, he would be there to protect you and investigate the disturbance. Essentially, he must prove beyond a doubt, he will be there for you. Don't give loyalty to a man who isn't committed to you, hoping he will be so enamored by your dedication that he will make you his woman. This exchange is taking place out of order. A man should first offer you reliability before you consider giving him any. Offering your loyalty prematurely doesn't make you "a ride or die chick," it makes you a silly chick.

When dating, choose a partner who mirrors your character and values. It is important to be with someone who loves the way you love. It is imperative that you take the time to make sure a man is capable of the same level of dependability you provide. You cannot force a man to match the effort you make in a relationship. This is why it is crucial to follow his lead and only contribute what he is contributing. Do not overexert yourself in a relationship and then get angry with a man for not giving as much as you. Allow him to meet you halfway to avoid giving a man too much. If making the distinction between a worthy and an unworthy man is difficult, make a conscious decision not to do or give more to him than he does or gives to you. This simple rule allows you to protect yourself until a man proves he is well-intentioned enough to deserve your loyalty.

KEEPING YOUR CROWN

KNOW EXACTLY WHO YOU ARE AND WHAT YOU WANT

When dating, women generally have a difficult time being honest about what they truly want. We often fear we are asking for too much and if we reveal our true intentions or expectations to a man, it will run him off. In some cases this is true. Although true, this should be reassuring. You unquestionably want to scare off the wrong men by being brutally honest about what you need to be happy. You have to make your wants and needs so crystal clear that you end up solely dealing with men who want the same things out of a relationship as you. For example, you can't pretend to "play it cool" or act as though you are content with a causal relationship when you actually want marriage or something serious. You are wasting your time by being dishonest about your intentions.

In addition to being honest with men about your needs, also make sure your demands and expectations are realistic and fair. Take a second to assess whether you have accurately determined what you have to offer. Are you underestimating or overestimating what you bring to the table and are you being totally self-aware? This is an important step toward understanding yourself, which will later simplify the process of finding a mate. Self-awareness is a prerequisite to finding a compatible life partner. Some women have a tendency to make outrageously long lists of characteristics they want from a partner, neglecting the fact that they themselves do not possess those same qualities. For example, some women insist they want a man who comes with "no baggage," yet they have children from previous relationships they expect a man to accept. Some women demand that their potential mate have a ridiculously great physique, yet they haven't stepped foot in a gym since junior high school. So, make sure your demands are fair and that you are not asking for attributes you do not provide. To ensure you do not have unrealistic demands, the following exercise will help you create a sensible list that will show you what qualities are reasonable to expect from your "Mr. Right."

First create a list of all the qualities and characteristics you are looking for in a partner. There is no limit to how long or short this list is, just make sure that it is comprised of your absolute "must-have" qualities. Divide your list of qualities you expect from your partner into three categories: physical attributes, character/personality traits, and lifestyle. Physical attributes include details such as height, build, race, age and style of dress. Character or personality traits include details such as a sense of humor, an outgoing personality, intellect, sensitivity and loyalty. Lifestyle attributes include whether he has children, his income, his level of education and his line of work. Now, let's analyze your list. First count the number of qualities you demand from your partner in each of the three categories. This will tell you which category is most important to you. If most of your characteristics fall under the physical attributes category, you may be too preoccupied with looks. This may be a sign of immaturity and an indication that you are not structuring your relationships with longevity in mind. Looks are guaranteed to fade. This indicates that you are not building your relationships on a solid foundation. If looks weigh this heavily in your decision making, you are probably not ready for something serious. However, if most of your attributes fall under the character/personality category, this is a promising sign.

KEEPING YOUR CROWN

Valuing a person's character is a more reliable indication that you are interested in finding a good person with whom you can develop a deep connection. In addition to having a compatible personality, ensure that the attributes under the lifestyle category are in alignment with your current or desired lifestyle. Having well-matched lifestyles and goals, accompanied by compatible personalities is the key to finding and maintaining a harmonious relationship and marriage that will last. Lastly, if your demands are spread relatively even among the three categories, your demands from a partner are well balanced. This is an indication of a healthy mindset and realistic expectations as long as the attributes you possess are evenly matched.

Now create a similar list of the attributes you feel you possess that add value to a relationship. It may be helpful to ask a close friend or family member to help you devise this list, considering it is often difficult to accurately gage or assess how we are perceived by others and what we actually offer in a relationship. Once again, divide your list of attributes into the same three categories. If the majority of your attributes fall under the physical category, you may be slightly one-dimensional. What you offer may lack substance and will likely only lead to short-term "flings." If the majority of your attributes fall under the character/personality category, this is an indication that you are capable of a deeper connection, however the attributes in your lifestyle category will further determine if you are ready for a life partner. Having good character will establish lifelong friendships but similarities in lifestyles and goals are also required to build the foundation for a healthy marriage.

Lastly, count the total number of qualities you demand from a partner and compare that with the total number of attributes you provide. If your list of expectations greatly outweighs what you offer, you may be asking for far too much. In this case, you need to analyze your list of demands and determine where you are "falling short" and work on making the attributes you provide more impressive. If you have high demands in the looks department but are not at your best physically, begin improving your appearance. If you have high demands from your ideal partner's lifestyle but are now realizing your lifestyle is not parallel or comparable, you need to either improve your lifestyle or adjust your demands and expectations from a potential mate. Conversely, if you are offering much more than you expect from a partner, you need to raise your expectations. You may also need to evaluate your level of confidence. Demanding less than you deserve is an indication of low self-worth. It is extremely dangerous to attempt to date or find love if you suffer from low self-esteem. In this case, you need to take a break from dating until you mend and address your internal issues to avoid being taken advantage of or wasting time entertaining prospects who are beneath you. However, if these two lists are similar in size and value, it is safe to assume your expectations are reasonable and justifiable and you possess enough self-awareness to find a compatible mate.

DON'T LOSE YOURSELF IN A RELATIONSHIP

After devising the list of attributes you provide, it is important to ask yourself "Do I offer enough?" Arriving at the answer to this question is necessary because it reveals whether you are even ready to date. Make sure you are whole and are not expecting another person to complete you or validate you. Make sure you are not lacking in so many areas that it results in you becoming needy, clingy or codependent. You cannot rely on someone else to create your happiness. It is a misconception to believe that having a man will make you happy or complete. This assumption is untrue and will leave you highly disappointed. Know yourself inside and out so you do not end up losing yourself in a relationship. You never want to become an extension of another person or end up deriving your identity from a relationship. Get yourself together before attempting to create a life with someone else.

Women often lose themselves in relationships and are clueless about how it even happened. Well ladies, this is how it happens: You meet a guy who is "just so perfect" and you convince yourself you are head over heels in love! You are committed to being the greatest girlfriend in the world! You cater to his every need by cooking, cleaning and doing other "wifely" duties. Because you want to spend every waking moment with your "perfect boyfriend," you fuse your social life with his. You are spending so much time in his social circle you completely neglect your friends. You make your social life all about him, his family and his friends. Then you take things a step further by attentively listening to his goals and dreams. You do everything you can to help him bring his dreams to fruition. Before you realize it, seeing him succeed has become your passion. You are his biggest fan! Your daily actions and efforts are now being directed toward helping him further his life. With your unyielding support, he is achieving his dreams. But this fantasy soon turns into a nightmare when he realizes his status and network has upgraded. Now that he is "the man" he is rubbing shoulders with a better caliber of people—and particularly women. He is now in a position to pursue women he never thought he could get. Landing one of these top-notch women will be the ultimate ego boost! In the event he can "pull" one of these women, he will "dropkick" your ass to the curb. You'll be alone, struggling to remember who you are and what you wanted out of life before you met this man. It will be difficult to recall what your wants and needs were before him. Then it hits you— the devastating realization that you have completely lost yourself in a relationship.

KEEPING YOUR CROWN

We have all witnessed this scenario where perhaps, a young woman commits to her college boyfriend, who later makes it to the league. She's supportive the entire time and once he "makes it" he now prefers to chase models and actresses. Men enjoy feeling as though they are "the man" and part of feeling like "the man" is having an impressive woman by his side. It strokes a man's ego to have nice "things." To leave the right impression, they'd rather show up in a Ferrari and not in a certified used Honda. So ladies, be a Ferrari not a used Honda. Mind you, this expression has nothing to do with a woman's physical appearance. Simply "looking good" doesn't make a woman a Ferrari. Ferraris are desirable because they are handcrafted and require time and specialized craftsmanship. Be the woman who has invested time and energy into herself and her life's passions which make her uniquely irresistible. Don't dull your shine while trying to be supportive of a man's dreams. Follow your own dreams and you'll be the girl some guy is chasing instead of being the loyal girlfriend a man is taking for granted.

Women should also understand that we often get in our own way by over-investing in insignificant, short-term relationships. In the previous scenario a woman made the mistake of placing her man "above her" which later motivated him to leave her behind. In many instances women over-invest in men with little or no ambition. Sometimes women fall in love with a man's "potential" and will inflate his ego while trying to motivate him to become the man she believes he is. A woman may invest in a man who is not ambitious at all. He may even be a loser. So, if a woman overvalues a man, he will believe he is better or more successful than he is, regardless of whether his lifestyle has improved. Women must realize how much influence they have in dictating a man's level of confidence. A woman can "make or break" a man's ego. It is possible to stroke a man's ego so hard or build him up so high, he will believe he is above you. This is why it is important for women to refrain from putting men on pedestals or overpraising them. Don't flatter a man so much that he thinks he can do better than you. Honestly, men don't need this level of dedication from you in these early stages of life. Just as you shouldn't take yourself too seriously in your younger years, don't take men too seriously either. This is the time in life to have fun, discover who you are and focus on your dreams.

To avoid losing yourself, you must focus on your life. Do not get so deep into a relationship that you forget who you are, what you like, what you need and what makes you happy. It is important for a woman to take a grace period, typically in her 20s, to find herself. You need this time to take risks, make mistakes, follow your dreams and achieve "something." This phase allows you to develop confidence and build self-respect. If you have truly nurtured this time in your life, it will be difficult for a man or anyone else to tell you who you are or who you aren't. Once you find yourself, it will be easy to avoid being emotionally or verbally abused by men. It's easier for a man to control a woman who doesn't have an identity or who has not established a trajectory for her life. Real men appreciate women who are passionate about their goals and have their identity intact. Underdeveloped men prefer women they can mold, change and control. When you commit to your dreams and goals, you will deter controlling or abusive men because you will intimidate them with your confidence and self-assurance.

Because this time in a woman's life is so crucial to her development, it is strongly advised that women wait until their late 20s or their 30s to get married. People change monumentally from one decade to the next. You are assuming a huge risk by interrupting this growth period and attempting to commit to someone when you are not yet the person you will become. A marriage will not bring you the joy you imagined if you jump into it before knowing who you are. There is an expression that says "getting married in your 20s is like leaving the club at 9:30." You have more to learn, do and experience. Don't limit your fun and ultimately your growth because you "jumped the gun." Once you survive your 20s it will be laughable to look back at how foolish you once were. If you've challenged yourself enough and have grown substantially, you may not even recognize your "old self." The silly relationships you placed so much emphasis on in your 20s, will look like child's play when you become a grown woman. Don't take yourself, your life or your relationships too seriously in this phase. Understand that this phase is about growth and self-awareness and look forward to becoming a smarter, more mature you. Know yourself from top to bottom. Know what you like to eat, what wine you enjoy, how you like to dress, what lifestyle you want for yourself, what type of people you enjoy being around, etc. It is especially important to arrive at a place where you thoroughly enjoy your alone time. There's a saying, "if you do not enjoy time alone, perhaps it is because you are not in good company." Make sure you are an independent person who can be happy alone and not the person who relies on a relationship to feel complete.

BE OPEN-MINDED

Once you have committed to being honest with yourself about what you want and have developed realistic expectations, the next step black women need to take to achieve a more fulfilling love life is to become more open-minded to interracial dating. We often limit our options by choosing to date black men exclusively but for various reasons—some justified and some unjustified—black men are not always as successful as black women. Black women are to be commended on their educational and entrepreneurial achievements. The number of black women who are business owners and CEOs or who are acquiring

Masters degrees and PhD's is impressive, to say the least. But the downside to being a successful black woman is that it is often difficult to find available black men who mirror the same lifestyle and level of success. If you deem it important to date and ultimately marry a man who is "equally yoked," you may need to broaden your options.

In addition to struggling to match our level of success, many black men are not marriage oriented and may not know how to be husbands. Because most black children are born to unwed mothers, many black men may not have witnessed a functioning marriage. They are often denied strong father figures and are consequently denied the teachings and examples of how to be good husbands. This dysfunction contributes to the black man's tendency to procreate outside of marriage. Many black men skip the marriage process and go straight to becoming a "baby daddy." If a woman is uninterested in becoming a stepmother, this arrangement may be undesirable—especially if his relationship with his "baby momma" is strained or tumultuous. If you are looking for a man who is marriage oriented, your odds of finding him will be higher if

KEEPING YOUR CROWN

you expand your options to include men who are not black as well. If you're ready for marriage, understand that it may be easier to date men from cultures that are more marriage oriented.

There is absolutely no need to compromise on any of the qualities and characteristics you look for in a partner, simply take race out of the equation. Having a partner who is compatible, evenly matched and who is kind to you is far more important than sacrificing these qualities so you can stay within your comfort zone. Ultimately, if your goal is to find true love, you can't stand in your own way by disregarding good men because they aren't black. Needless to say, there are countless systematic obstacles in place in this country that are intentional in making it difficult for black men to succeed. There are so many deeply woven layers to this problem that tackling this issue is beyond the scope of this book. So, until we can strengthen our community to a place where our men are no longer susceptible to sabotage, we must operate within our current reality. In the meantime, don't settle for a black man who doesn't treat you the way you deserve to be treated to avoid being alone.

In addition to being open to interracial dating, be open-minded to alternative ways of finding love by giving online dating a try. In this day in age, people are busier than ever. Luckily, technology has provided a practical solution to finding a mate. Although online dating once had a stigma for being a place for weirdos to find love, it is now a realistic and useful solution to finding a compatible mate. There are several companies that appeal to successful people who are serious about finding love so don't be afraid to give it a chance. If you are in a place in your life where you are ready to give and receive love, be open-minded enough to give yourself the prospects you deserve.

BE NICE

This may sound remedial or like advice a mother would give her child but unfortunately some black women forget, when dating, it is only appropriate to be respectful and nice. As grown women, we may endure BS at work or throughout the day but it is completely unacceptable to bring that negative energy with you on a date. Understand that life is not necessarily easy for men either—and especially for black men. So bringing your problems with you to a social outing is out-of-line and is totally unnecessary. Dating is simply an opportunity to have fun and get to know the other person better. Also keep in mind, a date is in some ways, an investment for men. Yes, you are lending your time and company but they are lending their time, company and money. So being an "angry black woman" because you had a bad day or are dissatisfied with the date is inappropriate and mean. Women are often hopeful that every encounter or every date will lead them to their husband. This is unrealistic. Prior to meeting "the one," you will meet many men who may not be compatible with you. This is no excuse to treat a man as if he is wasting your time. Be nice and polite anyway. It is likely that although a particular man may not be the man for you, he could end up becoming a great friend. This is not an implication that if a man is rude or disrespectful, you should stick around and be mistreated. However, if he is respectful, but not "your type," make an effort to enjoy the date and have a good time regardless of whether this man is your soulmate.

KEEPING YOUR CROWN

Having a fulfilling love life is important because it adds value to a woman's life. However, it is crucial that we ensure our relationships enhance our quality of life. When relationships become counterproductive to our happiness and growth, we must reevaluate our habits and make adjustments to improve our chances for finding true happiness. Many black women are loyal to a fault in relationships. We must understand that although we are naturally dedicated women, it is only necessary to give our loyalty to men who are devoted to us. Allow men to meet you half way and never give a man more effort than he is giving you. Also understand the importance of being self-aware when dating. Know what value you add to a relationship and create demands that are reasonable and fair based on what you provide. Make sure you are ready to date prior to looking for companionship. Make sure you invest in yourself, your dreams, your wants and needs so you do not lose yourself in a relationship. To give yourself the prospects you deserve, be more open-minded to finding love. Give interracial dating and online dating a chance and always remember to be nice. Every encounter may not necessarily lead you to the man of your dreams but be nice anyway. When applying these concepts, it will be easier to achieve productive dating experiences which will lead to meaningful relationships!

SECTION ONE: CHALLENGE TO OUR QUEENS

- Be selective with your loyalty. Allow men to meet you half way. Do not do more for a man than he does for you.
- Perform an honest self-assessment to get a clear understanding of what you offer in a relationship and establish realistic demands from a partner.
- Avoid getting married too young. Understand that your 20s are the time to learn, grow and invest in yourself to avoid losing yourself in a relationship.
- Stop overinvesting in short-term relationships in your younger years and spend your youth focusing on yourself, your wants, your needs and your goals.

KEEPING YOUR CROWN

- Broaden your options for potential prospects by eliminating race from your criteria and perhaps, give online dating a try.

SECTION TWO:
UNDERSTANDING MEN

Women are to be Loved, Men are to be Understood · Understanding a Man's Purpose · Let Men Pursue You · Don't Let Men Dictate the Way You Feel About the Way You Look

2

SECTION TWO:
UNDERSTANDING MEN

"What I notice about men, all men, is that their order is me, my family, God is in there somewhere, but me is first." –Michelle Obama

This will be one of the shortest chapter in this book considering men are extremely simple, contrary to what most women believe. Conversely, it would require an entire book or perhaps even a series of books to analyze or understand women. Let's face it; women are an incredibly complex species. Men on the other hand, only need three things to be happy: (1) Validation- A man needs to feel as if he is "the man." He needs to have his ego stroked, so it's crucial to tell him when he is doing a good job. Remember, there is a difference between validation and overpraising. Validation is necessary but overpraising is dangerous. Also, never, ever emasculate a man unless you want him to leave you because that is exactly what he will do. (2) Space- A man needs space to breath. Men find it terribly obnoxious when a woman is incessantly clingy. Allow him to enjoy time away from you, with his friends, without you hounding and interrogating him as if you are his mother. If there are certain hobbies or activities a man enjoys and has enjoyed prior to knowing you, it is important that you respect the time he delegates to these activities that make him happy. If he enjoys fixing cars or watching sports, respect his happiness and allow him to do so. (3) Regular Sex. This is self-explanatory but men need sex. Make sure you "take care" of your man regularly. Allowing your man to be "strained up" might be risky because he may become susceptible to temptation. In a nutshell, tending to these few needs will keep a man happy and content. Keep in mind it is only necessary to fulfill these three needs for a man who has earned your effort such as your husband or a man who has husband potential. Trying to fulfill these needs for every man is unnecessary and is a waste of your time.

… KEEPING YOUR CROWN

WOMEN ARE TO BE LOVED, MEN ARE TO BE UNDERSTOOD

When dealing with men, the most important factor to realize is that a woman must understand her man. Ultimately, women need to be loved and men need to be understood. Whether they know it or not, men value being understood more than being loved. Loving a man without understanding him will only get a woman so far. We often hear women proclaim, "But I loved him the most!" after he leaves her for a woman who appears less invested. Men do not need to be "over-loved," they need to be understood. In fact, most men stray because another woman was willing to listen to him objectively to better understand him and his needs. The "other woman" did not tell him how to feel or behave, she simply accepted him for who he is and allowed him to be himself. By understanding what a man values (what he likes or dislikes, what turns him on or off, what makes him feel good about himself, and what makes him vulnerable) a woman has the power to make him feel so acknowledged and special, he will fall in love with her. Also, by understanding a man's vulnerabilities and breaking points, a woman can avoid unintentionally breaking a man's trust. This is important because, unlike women, men rarely give second chances when a person breaks their trust. When a woman realizes the power that comes with totally understanding a man, she is able to keep him completely satisfied. So keep in mind, a woman is better off understanding her man rather than being hopelessly in love or infatuated with him. For men, receiving love is not regarded as highly as being understood.

However, understanding a man should not be used as a tactic to force an incompatible relationship to work. It should simply be a way for women to improve the functionality of a healthy and well-matched relationship. For instance, don't pretend to be a domestic goddess because a man likes to be catered to at home, if you are actually a working woman who despises being domestic. These inconsistencies reveal a compatibility issue, not a failure on your part to understand his needs. In this case you should confront why you are forcing this relationship to work. In a healthy relationship, fulfilling a man's needs should also make you happy and should allow you to be true to who you are. If you find yourself in a relationship in which satisfying a man's needs is making you unhappy, you need to move on.

Men are simple and their likes and needs are decipherable. Women on the other hand, are complicated and don't even know what they want half the time. This is why women are to be loved. Unconditional love is the only emotion that will make a woman's erratic behavior tolerable. However, a woman can love a man until she is blue in the face and it won't mean a thing to him if she doesn't understand him and how to fulfill his needs. Women waste a lot of time and energy loving men too hard, when essentially all a man needs is for a woman to understand him and how to satisfy his three needs— validation, space and sex. It is beneficial for women to grasp this concept because it is much easier to understand a man than it is to shower him with love he never demanded or needed. So commit to the man who loves you the most and make it a point to understand him fully.

KEEPING YOUR CROWN

UNDERSTANDING A MAN'S PURPOSE

Women tend to have overly romanticized ideals of what a man should be. The truth of the matter is, in addition to loving her, men are to play two major roles in a woman's life. He should be a protector and a provider. As the physically stronger sex, generally speaking, a man is expected to keep his woman safe and out of harm's way. Furthermore, he should insist on performing simple, chivalrous acts like opening doors for you and maintaining the outside position when walking down the street. As a provider he should make your life more comfortable. The days when men were the sole providers are long gone. Today, women are more than capable of being financially self-sufficient. Although many women are providing for themselves, if a man is present he should add to his woman's level of comfortability. For instance, if a man is present, a woman should not tackle her car maintenance, house maintenance or yard work alone. When a man is fulfilling these and other cardinal duties, his presence will be felt and it will be unarguably apparent that her life is improved by his involvement. It is a man's responsibility to ensure that his woman does not forgo any of the resources she needs to be safe and happy. This is a man's purpose in your life. Respect this role and do not try to assume a man's position, unless of course, you are a lesbian providing for another woman.

Once you understand a man's role it becomes easy to respect his position and live harmoniously together. Women need to dispel the ridiculous expectations that have been placed on men such as expecting them to be mind-readers, expecting them to pay attention to menial and irrelevant details (like remembering to put the toilet seat down), expecting them to listen to and enjoy gossip and expecting them to give you self-esteem. So, do not overvalue men. Women must stop putting men on pedestals and developing unrealistic expectations for them that they are incapable of achieving. Women need to grow up and stop worshiping men as if they are knights in shining armor from their favorite childhood fairytale. Although having a good man will truly compliment your life, men are not magical miracle workers. With this in mind, be sure not to undervalue a man's role in your life. If a man loves you, makes you feel safe and secure and is adding value to your life, be gracious and make sure he knows he is appreciated. The goal is to better understand him and his role and develop realistic expectations.

Furthermore, as a woman you are responsible for knowing what you want out of life, what makes you happy and where you are trying to go. Do not allow a man to influence or dictate your goals or direction in life because (1) it is not his responsibility and (2) ultimately it will not make you happy. Make sure you make taking care of yourself a top priority. Men more than adequately look out for themselves and you should do the same. It is not necessary or logical for you to "look out" for him, while he's "looking out" for him. Who is going to "look out" for you? In order for a relationship to function, there must be two complete people present. When a woman focuses on her happiness and goals, she will become a more desirable partner. When you are working toward improving your life, you automatically improve your partnership. When you are looking out for self, the way men do, the relationship will naturally have balance. Both parties will be content and happy and can live harmoniously together. Good men are in a sense, "assets" that can greatly assist women on their journey to happiness. However, don't confuse this with the notion that simply having a man will make you happy.

LET MEN PURSUE YOU

It goes without saying, men and women are "wired" substantially different. We have different needs and different factors that drive and motivate us. One particular pleasure men enjoy is the thrill of the chase. In addition to enjoying the chase, their testosterone gives them the confidence to endure rejection without a loss of enthusiasm. In fact, it is often resistance or the challenge that excites them and motivates them to try harder. Unlike men, women are not wired this way and should never offer themselves to a man and allow him the option of saying yea or nay. Women are to be pursued and should allow men to fulfill their role as the pursuer. Men are extremely decisive about what attracts them and who they want to pursue. Therefore, as a woman, your dating candidates are to be drawn from the pool of men who are actively pursuing you. Keep in mind, if you are not impressed with the caliber of men who are pursuing you, you might need to "step your game up," considering you are who you attract. To attract better men, you need to work on becoming a better woman. Furthermore, a woman should never consider a man who is not pursuing her and she most certainly should not consider a man who isn't even interested in her. This is as useless as waiting to receive a job offer from a company that never granted you an interview. A woman should only entertain the men who are properly courting her and eventually, if she chooses, she can commit to the man that is exerting the most effort to win her heart.

With this in mind, it is important for women to understand that when single, a woman should date multiple men from the pool of men who are pursuing her. Never feel guilty about dating multiple men. Women have a tendency to give time and attention to one man, only to endure disappointment when things do not work out. It is likely that the men you are entertaining are dating multiple women, so it makes complete sense for you to do the same. Dating multiple men will also lessen your desire to interrogate a man about other women he may be dating—

KEEPING YOUR CROWN

which is totally inappropriate and unattractive. Simply enjoy attention and courtship from all the prospects that interest you.

When dating multiple men, consider this process a way of determining who likes you the most according to their efforts. Ultimately, you want to narrow down your prospects to find a good man who is nice to you. This process encourages women to entertain "nice guys" who treat them well. However, there are many women who insist they dislike "nice guys." These women assert that nice men are boring and instead they prefer men who are "assholes" because they enjoy the challenge. A woman may convince herself that if she can get a mean man to be nice to her, his change in disposition signifies how special she is and how deeply he loves her. This desire to change a bad man into a good man is irrational and indicates questionable self-worth. If you feel you need to "change" a man to feel validated, you don't love yourself enough. If a woman considers a man who mistreats her appealing, this indicates immaturity and an underdeveloped mind-set. Mature women who love themselves expect to be treated well. In addition, men who are marriage material know how to treat women well and will eventually make great husbands and fathers. So, don't waste your time ignoring nice guys to chase thugs and players, hoping you can change them into marriage material. The idea of dating a thug might seem cute until he gets you pregnant with no intentions of marrying you, starts cheating on you, gets physical with you when confronted about his infidelity and eventually leaves you and his child with no remorse.

Some women refute the philosophy of letting a man pursue them because they prefer to chase high profile men with "swag." They'd rather chase a man who has multiple women vying for his attention, believing that landing this type of man will somehow establish her worth or place her "above" other women. However, this way of thinking is preposterous because again, women should not pursue men, competing for a man is childish and snagging a high profile man does not make you "better" than other women. When a woman joins a pool of women who are competing for one man, she devalues herself by blending in with the rest of his groupies. Even if a woman outperforms all the other groupies and "wins" the title of being his woman, a man will not regard her very highly if he did not have to earn her heart. As a man, he derives more satisfaction from competing for and winning his woman rather than electing the groupie who worked the hardest to win a superficial title. Regardless of a man's status, it is not a woman's role to worship or shamelessly pursue a man.

Allow men to compete unknowingly with one another for you. Eventually one man will exert more effort than the others. At this point you can entertain the idea of giving him exclusivity IF AND ONLY IF he specifically asks you to be his woman. It is a huge mistake to claim a man simply because you chose to date him exclusively. Once again, men are incredibly simple. If they want to commit to you and only you, they will ask you. Assuming a man is yours because he calls you, texts you, took you out one time or has sex with you, is simply not true and will only end in heartache. Simply put, here are the rules: (1) under no circumstances should a woman ever pursue a man or even consider a man who is not interested in her and (2) do not become smitten by a man's initial efforts. Courtship is a process. Give him the necessary time to either screw up or prove he is sincerely interested in you before you "catch feelings." This grace period spares you from disappointment and is much more enjoyable when you have other prospects you are "juggling." This is why courtship is so important and essential. It is imperative that women let men pursue them. Men like what they like and a woman cannot change a man's mind about what he likes. A woman cannot cook her way, sex her way, buy her way or beg her way into a man's heart. It CANNOT be done. Ladies, let men pursue you. Chase your dreams, not men!

"If a man wants you, nothing can keep him away. If he doesn't want you, nothing can make him stay." –
Oprah Winfrey

DON'T LET MEN DICTATE HOW YOU FEEL ABOUT THE WAY YOU LOOK

It is a known fact that men are extremely visual and being visually appealing is the quickest way to get a man's attention, initially. Because of this, women have a tendency to get wrapped up in trying to become physically attractive to men. We've all seen the woman who puts effort into her appearance to get a man and then "let's herself go" while in the relationship. Then once the relationship ends, she's back to being high-maintenance again. This is the most common scenario in which a woman allows a man to dictate how much effort she puts into her appearance. A woman must set a personal standard for how she wants to represent herself and how well she treats herself. This standard must be completely unrelated to a man's influence. Routine grooming, such as manicures, pedicures, shaving, waxing and hair appointments should be performed out of self-love to show appreciation for yourself and your body. The sole motivation for grooming should not be for a man's approval or to get a man. Although men will undoubtedly appreciate it, we must value our bodies and treat physical upkeep as a gift to ourselves. Also, there is absolutely nothing wrong with preferring a low maintenance lifestyle. It is completely acceptable to have little desire to perform many of the previously mentioned grooming practices. Ultimately, it is important to look and feel the way you want, regardless of what men may think.

It is also not uncommon for a woman to undergo extreme cosmetic surgery procedures, hoping it will make her more enticing to men. This is a huge mistake. There is a distinct difference between "attention" and "attraction." Getting the "porn star package" which includes outrageous lip injections, hips injections, butt injections and large breast implants will undoubtedly grab a man's attention. It's not every day you see a living, breathing, walking blow up doll. This may make a man's head turn but don't be fooled. This is not the type of woman a respectable man would introduce to his mother. As a queen you should only desire attention from respectable men. Any "man" who finds a woman with a "build-a-body" suitable to be his woman is lacking masculinity. He thrives off of the attention she demands to prove to everyone that he is "the man." Perhaps he desperately needs her overt sexuality to establish the illusion that he is heterosexual. Insecure men, who are compensating for a lack of confidence in their "manhood," often prefer women who look like sex. Don't waste your time trying to appeal to an insecure man. You will find yourself highly disappointed with his inability to satisfy you anyway. Ultimately, real men desire respectable women. They are attracted to women who carry themselves well and leave something to the imagination. Real men are quite possessive over women they care for and respect. They prefer women who exude femininity without misrepresenting or disrespecting themselves. So although we live in a generation that often encourages women to look like they work in the sex industry, respect yourself and do not allow misguided influences to dictate your definition of beauty. It is imperative that women make a conscious decision to look the way they want to look. Make sure the effort you put into your appearance is for you, first and foremost. The opinion that carries the most weight concerning your appearance is your own. As a queen, always exude confidence and look good for you because you love and respect yourself. Ultimately, confidence is the quality men find most attractive anyway.

Women must realize how incredibly simple men are. Once women stop overcomplicating the male psyche, they will realize men need very little to be satiated in a relationship. Women need to relax, stop overexerting themselves and understand how to best satisfy her man's three needs—validation, space and sex. Women must not overvalue or undervalue a man's purpose in her life. It is a man's responsibility to love us, protect us and provide for us. Women must eliminate unrealistic expectations placed on men to avoid setting themselves up for disappointment. It is crucial that women allow men to pursue them. Men like what they like and a woman cannot change what a man likes, regardless of how hard she tries. So, only consider men who are actively pursuing you and date multiple men while single. Love yourself and do not allow men to dictate how you feel concerning your appearance. Your appearance is an expression of who you are, so don't allow a man to influence your idea of beauty.

SECTION TWO: CHALLENGE TO OUR QUEENS

- **Exert more effort into understanding a man. This will serve you more than loving him hopelessly.**

- **While single, date more than one man. Dating is sometimes a "numbers game." Allow men to unknowingly compete for you to increase your chances of finding a kind and loving partner.**

KEEPING YOUR CROWN

- Wait until a man offers you exclusivity before you claim him! Claiming a man prematurely will likely end in heartbreak and humiliation.
- Men are the pursuers and women are to be pursued. Allow a man to court you and never chase a man.
- Don't let men dictate the way you look. Look good for you because you love, value and respect yourself.

SECTION THREE:
MANAGING HOW WE TREAT EACH OTHER

What Type of Woman Are You? · How to Handle Your Thoughts and Judgements · How to Handle Judgement When you're on the Receiving End

3

SECTION THREE:
MANAGING HOW WE TREAT EACH OTHER

"Why can't women get along? Because we're afraid. We're afraid to be vulnerable. We're afraid to be soft. We're afraid to be hurt. But most of all, we're afraid of our power. So we become controlling and aggressive and vicious." –Iyanla Vanzant

While on the path to realizing and accepting our position as queens, we must understand the importance of how we interact with and treat other black women. Our journey as black women is distinctly ours. We have obstacles and issues only we know and understand. Having a sisterhood that is nurturing, accepting and supportive is imperative. It is difficult to comprehend, considering what we have been through as a race, why some black people still struggle with the idea of comradery. The "crabs in a bucket" theory is often used to describe the lack of unification black people possess. This has to stop if we ever want to advance our communities to a place that is more reflective of our beautiful and resilient heritage. Women are much more influential in change than we may know or believe. On the path to rebuilding our communities we must first start with ourselves and the way we treat our sisters.

The following categories describe three different types of women in relation to how they treat other women. Keep in mind, the role we play in our interactions with other women is often subconscious. We are typically unaware of how we are perceived, what judgements we assume, what offends us, and what intimidates us. When dealing with each other, a woman's behavioral tendencies usually fall into one of the following categories: (1) The "Confident Woman" (2) The Woman with "Conditional-Confidence" and (3) The "Woman-Hater." Before placing yourself in a category, read each description to see if there are any behavioral parallels with which you can identify. The point of this exercise is not to establish some sort of hierarchy among women. The objective is to have a moment of complete honesty with yourself which may bring awareness to any underlying issues you may possess. This is important so you can better understand yourself and build upon any areas that need improvement to become a better woman and a better sister to your fellow queens.

WHAT TYPE OF WOMAN ARE YOU?

The "Confident Woman": The confident woman truly loves herself. She knows herself inside and out. She knows both her strengths and weaknesses and she is okay with them. She derives her value from internal qualities, such as her character, her compassion, her intellect and her sense of humor. She is incapable of being intimidated by another woman's physical appearance or achievements because she is secure with who she is at her core. She does not compare herself to other women and is truly happy to see other women succeed. When interacting with other women she is sincerely open to making a connection. She has no pretense or judgements towards other women based on superficial assumptions. Her opinions of other women are based on what she has learned or experienced as a result of interacting with them. She is generally kind, understanding that how she treats others is a reflection of her character, not theirs.

The woman with "Conditional-Confidence": This woman can appear to be the "confident woman." She may have great posture, a great handshake and appears to have it all together until she feels threatened with competition. This facade shatters the second she thinks another woman can provide or is providing the same attributes she offers. Essentially, she feels threatened by any woman she believes "can replace her." For example, if a woman with "conditional-confidence" leads with her intellect and derives her identity from her smarts and accomplishments, when interacting with another smart woman, the woman with "conditional-confidence" will respond with passive-aggressive hostility and competitiveness. She will try to "out-smart" her "competition" every chance she gets. Similarly, a woman who leads with her physical beauty or sexuality will feel threatened by other beautiful or sexy women. Women who derive their identity from motherhood may exert superiority over women who are not mothers or may condemn women they believe are bad moms. The woman with "conditional-confidence" needs her peers to believe she is the more intelligent woman, the sexier woman or the better mother so her identity can remain intact. However, competing with other women actually provides the opposite effect. Instead of masking her insecurities, she is now magnifying them.

If you realize you're a woman who is constantly threatened by women who are similar to you, your love for self may be more "egoic" than sincere. "Egoic" defined by spiritual teacher, Eckhart Tolle, is the voice in your head you mistake for your actual self, which is conditioned by your past, your upbringing, your identification with possessions and other worldly identifiers that have little to do with who you actually are. In other words, you have created a false identity for yourself that you fear another woman can destroy. You identify yourself by worldly accomplishments such as your career, your house, your car, your husband and other people's perceptions of you, thus making your identity fragile and easily challenged.

KEEPING YOUR CROWN

To grow into the "confident woman" and leave your "conditional-confidence" behind, you must realize you are doing yourself a huge disservice by believing in and trying to preserve false identities. The woman with "conditional-confidence" must attempt to recognize these negative and competitive thoughts as they surface. She must form a habit of dispelling these thoughts as they occur. She must become conscious of the fact that a "win" for one black woman is essentially a "win" for us all. She must resist the urge to compete with women who share her same attributes and instead perceive these similarities as common ground and an opportunity to bond. Our talents will go further when we network and form a sisterhood with women who have common strengths as opposed to competing with one another. The woman with "conditional-confidence" must also place more value on her character and less value on superficial, worldly achievements. Once you understand your true self better, you learn there is a sense of uniqueness about you that no one else can possess or replace. Your true self is infinitely more beautiful and loveable than any facade will ever be and thus cannot be challenged or destroyed. True self-love begins when you understand and adore who you are at your core—flaws and all. When you truly fall in love with yourself, seeing others shine will never challenge your identity or position.

The woman with no confidence aka, the "Woman-Hater": The "woman-hater" finds very little she likes about herself. There may be various reasons for this discontentment with self. Some "woman-haters" may have experienced verbal abuse, either from their childhood or sometimes from toxic relationships in adulthood. Some "woman-haters" do not have relationships with their fathers and in turn, suffer from low self-esteem. Her longing for male attention or "daddy-issues" causes her to overvalue men and therefore view ALL women as competition. The "women-hater" is generally unhappy with her overall life (her job, her relationship, her lack of a relationship, her physical appearance, etc.). Instead of coming to terms with her low self-esteem and trying to better herself, she subconsciously projects how she feels about herself onto other women. You'll often find the "woman-hater" cutting her eyes at other women and giving them dirty looks. She constantly has rude and judgmental opinions about complete strangers as though they were her enemy. Having such strong convictions about strangers is a clear indication that her real problem is with herself. Happy people are kind and light-hearted. We've all heard the expression "hurt people hurt people" and this sentiment is clearly true for the "woman-hater."

"We really don't know how to love each other because we haven't really learned to love ourselves. In many instances, not all, it's not malicious. We've just been conditioned to such bad behavior." –Iyanla Vanzant

To change yourself from a "woman-hater" to the "confident woman" you must figure out what you need to be happy. There are five changes the "woman-hater" can implement to find happiness: (1) be nicer (2) have more gratitude (3) mend your internal issues (4) improve your physical appearance and (5) start having sex.

Be Nicer: Regardless of your circumstance, every individual has the power to control how they respond to life's challenges. One immediate way to start feeling better about yourself and your life is by being nice. When you are in a bad mood, having a bad day or are in a low place in life, it doesn't feel good to be mean. One can only dispel negativity by combating it with positivity. The "woman-hater" must work on being nice to people. Generally speaking, we are all good people at our core, so when we lash out, behave ugly, or disrespect people it makes us feel bad about ourselves. We experience shame when we behave in ways that are dishonorable or when we display behavior we are not proud of. Sure, it is easy to conduct ourselves poorly when we don't feel good about life but being mean is not the answer. The most immediate way to feel good is by being kind and performing kind acts. If you are a "woman-hater" who needs to boost her moral, start by being nice and watch how much better it will make you feel about yourself!

Have More Gratitude: In order to find happiness, the "woman-hater" must also work on having gratitude. It is crucial to start being grateful for the blessings we already have. It is important for unhappy people to approach life with a more gracious and positive outlook. Start each morning by reciting to yourself the things you are grateful for. Also, while performing daily tasks that irritate you, try interrupting your usual negative thoughts with thoughts of gratitude. Be grateful for dirty dishes because they are an indication that you have food to eat. If your husband irritates you, try to acknowledge his positive qualities and what he contributes to your life. If you hate your job, be grateful for an income. It is completely acceptable to look for a better job in the meantime but having gratitude for your current circumstance will yield positive energy that will attract better opportunities. Be grateful for your health, your family and your friends. Find a new appreciation for the little things in life you may take for granted. One sure way to create happiness is by acknowledging and appreciating the blessings you already have.

Mend Your Internal Issues: If your unhappiness stems from a lifelong battle of dealing with low self-esteem, resulting from childhood trauma such as an absent parent or parents or enduring abuse, you need to seek counseling. Receiving advice from a professional is the first step to overcoming your low self-worth and reclaiming your happiness. If your relationship is weighing you down or negatively affecting your self-esteem, now is the time to confront it. Be honest about what you need to be happy. If you can mend the relationship with counseling then do so. If the relationship is damaged beyond repair, have the courage to end it. If a great deal of your sadness stems from not having companionship, be proactive in building a love life. Online dating is a great place to start. The in-depth compatibility assessments are effective at matching you with someone with similar values and interests. If online dating doesn't interest you, ask close friends or family members to play match-maker and become more open-minded and optimistic when getting to know new people.

Improve Your Physical Appearance: Mending your internal issues is more than half the battle on the road to becoming the "confident-woman." Being whole internally will help you love yourself and reclaim your happiness. If you have tackled your internal insecurities and still experience discontentment with your physical appearance, this should be the next step on your path to self-improvement. If you are a "woman-hater" who is mean to or offended by women you believe look better than you, it is your responsibility to stop comparing yourself and start improving yourself. The upside to tackling this aspect of your self-esteem is that you are solely responsible for your progress. Unlike overcoming internal problems, which require help from outside influences, improving your physical appearance is predominantly within your control. So be honest with yourself about what aspects of your physical appearance you are unhappy with and be proactive in improving them. This is the time to kick your discipline level up a notch. If you aren't happy with your weight, get that long overdue gym membership and improve your diet. If you are unhappy with the way your breasts look, begin saving for the breast augmentation you've always wanted. Do what you must to feel great about your physical appearance! Furthermore, focusing on improving your physical appearance forces you to become preoccupied with self instead of being consumed with how other women look.

"Comparison is an act of violence against the self." –Iyanla Vanzant

KEEPING YOUR CROWN

Start Having Sex: One common problem the "woman-hater" possesses is a lack of intimacy. This may sound crazy but is true nevertheless. By design, women are loving and sensitive and need attention and affection. Women who lack affection or are deprived of meaningful or enjoyable sex, are mean and angry. This lack of intimacy can create built up anger and bitterness. Having a healthy sex life relieves stress, improves your mood and your overall quality of life! It is your responsibility as a woman to take ownership of your sex life. There are no specific rules on how to jumpstart your sex life, but here are a few dos and don'ts for establishing a fulfilling sex life. Select a casual sex partner who respects you and your privacy. The last thing you should have to worry about is someone divulging your personal business or disrespecting you. DO NOT sleep with men who are involved! Under no circumstance is this acceptable. Also make sure you use discretion when choosing your sexual partner. Avoid sleeping with men you would be uncomfortable seeing regularly such as your boss, co-workers, neighbors, close "friends," etc. Try to avoid sleeping with men who "run in the same circles." Specifically, do not sleep with two different men who are friends or associates or men who have friends or associates in common. Ultimately, you do not want to be labeled as a "jump-off" or a "homie-hopper." Keep some distance between your casual sex partners. Women may think it is acceptable to be as sexually reckless as men. This is not necessarily true because ultimately women will endure more scrutiny than men for the same behavior. This is clearly a double standard but women are expected to uphold higher standards for how we treat our bodies. Always practice safe sex. Your intention is to enjoy yourself, not to end up at the clinic or end up becoming his next baby momma—not fun at all! Younger men are great candidates for casual sex partners because more often than not, they are great at pleasing you sexually, while demanding little-to-nothing in return. These are general guidelines for enhancing or establishing a happy sex life. The most is important aspect is to know yourself and what you can or cannot handle within your intimate relationships to create an enjoyable and stress free sex life.

KEEPING YOUR CROWN

BE AWARE OF YOUR THOUGHTS AND JUDGEMENTS

In social settings in the future, pay attention to your thoughts and feelings as you engage with other women. Be aware of how you respond to certain types of women. Take note of your internal dialogue. When you see a beautiful woman, what do you think to yourself about her? Does the way you feel about how you look at that moment change? Does your confidence level change or remain the same? Are your judgements about her based on her actions and behavior or based on your own preconceived-notions? Do the same exercise when engaging any type of woman who ignites an emotional response within you. Take a mental note of these responses because they will tell you a lot about how you feel about yourself. These responses will show you what areas of your self-image lack confidence and in what areas you feel self-assured. Once you build up the areas of your self-esteem that need attention and tackle your insecurities, you'll find yourself becoming a happier and kinder person. When you are being present and self-aware, you bring your best self—free of judgement and criticism—

to social interactions with other women. This allows you to become sincerely kind to other women and kind to yourself.

HOW TO HANDLE JUDGEMENT WHEN YOU ARE ON THE RECEIVING END

Once you've done the work required to love and accept yourself and have learned to appreciate and respect other women, you may find yourself on the receiving end of judgement and jealously from other women. This is a great opportunity to practice compassion and patience. Never take sideways looks or passive-aggressive insults from other women personal. Remove your emotions from the situation. Before becoming defensive or offended, understand that the problem this woman has is personal and is none of your business. Her issue is with herself and not with you. At this point it is your responsibility to respond with either grace or kindness or simply do not respond at all. Any woman who displays disgraceful and immature behavior is insecure and unhappy. As a strong "confident woman," you realize this and understand there is no victory to gain by beating down someone who is already beat down. Be the example of how

KEEPING YOUR CROWN

a queen conducts herself by taking the high road and always carry yourself with class and respect.

It is important for women to recognize how sensitive we all are. We are often hard enough on ourselves and are our own toughest critics. We often harshly judge our own appearance, our accomplishments, our level of success, our children's level of success, etc. There is no need to be mean to other women, considering women are already so hard on themselves. In addition to the outrageous standards we hold ourselves to, we often have to deal with being overlooked, undermined and objectified in society and in the workplace. So it is important for women to establish comradery and a support system to alleviate and combat the adversity we encounter, instead of treating each other poorly. Understand that women who are the meanest are often the most hurt. Although it may be difficult to rationalize their behavior in that moment, it is more appropriate to utilize empathy and compassion when dealing with mean women. You may never know what another woman is going through or what issues she is battling. So try to be kind when dealing with each other.

SECTION THREE: CHALLENGE TO OUR QUEENS

- You are not your car, your career, your marriage or any other worldly identifiers. Don't confuse what you have for who you are. Love yourself truly and unconditionally.
- Stop comparing yourself to other women. Your journey is your own. When you compete with other women, instead of masking your insecurities, you magnify them.
- Work on improving your internal issues and your physical discontentment. Only concern yourself with being at your best mentally, physically and spiritually.
- If you are mean and angry due to a lack of intimacy, find a suitable casual sex partner and relieve your built-up frustrations to become a kinder person.
- Understand the value of comradery among your fellow queens. Treat yourself and other black women with the upmost respect.

SECTION FOUR:
CHANGING OUR VIEWS ON SINGLE MOTHERHOOD

How Single Motherhood is Perceived · The Effects on Your Child · How "Daddy Issues" are Destroying "Black Love" · Remember, Your Child is not Your Friend · How Your Decision to Date Affects Your Child · The Single Exception to Single Motherhood · Oops! I'm A Baby Momma...What Now?

4

SECTION FOUR:
CHANGING OUR VIEWS ON SINGLE MOTHERHOOD

"A stable and nurturing childhood is essential for the healthy psycho-emotional and spiritual development of a human being. While we may understand what is supposed to happen to us physically, we must begin to better understand what happens to children mentally, emotionally and spiritually as a result of the families into which they are born." –Iyanla Vanzant

Black women can single-handedly improve the condition of the black community by repairing the black family structure. Strong and stable black families are the foundation for healthy and successful black communities. Black women have a direct influence on how black families are created and must regard family and legacy with the upmost importance.

It has become increasingly common that black women are deciding to tackle motherhood alone. According to the 2015 U.S. Census Bureau, 72 percent of black children are born out of wedlock and raised in single parent households. This number is alarming, especially considering Asians only make up 17 percent and white children make up 29 percent. More than any other race, black women make up the majority of single mothers. Black women are getting married much less than other demographics but are continuing to have children, nonetheless. Black women are so accustomed to single motherhood it has sadly become our norm or status quo. This dysfunctional family structure is so common it is often recreated in media advertisements. For instance, when families are portrayed in television commercials, white, Hispanic and Asian families are pictured having the full family structure—which consists of a husband, a wife and their children. However, black women are often depicted as the single mother with children, absent of a husband. This portrayal is not at the fault of the media. It simply reflects what has become far too prevalent in our communities. This has to stop. Black women must redefine "what is normal." Although single motherhood is incredibly common and some find it permissible, under no circumstance is it acceptable. The truth of the matter is, this is not the best way to start a family. Although black women are tenacious enough to manage juggling their education and career while raising children alone, this is not the ideal environment for creating well-adjusted children, nor is it safe for a woman to raise a child alone.

The topic of being a baby momma is analyzed so infrequently that single mothers are unaware to what extent single motherhood damages our community. This is largely attributable to the fact that most single mothers were raised by single mothers. Naturally one single mother won't judge another single mother for making similar decisions. However, regardless of the fact that single mothers are not judging each other, black women need to understand the negative perceptions associated with being a baby momma and the negative effects single motherhood has on both our children and our community. We'll specifically discuss how baby mommas are perceived from the viewpoint of: (1) their baby daddy (2) their potential future prospects and (3) society. Many people may argue that being concerned with how others view you is unimportant but as queens, we most certainly should care to some degree, how we are perceived. We should hold ourselves to high standards and be conscious of the fact that the life choices we make paint a picture of who we are. We should want this picture to represent us in a positive light.

HOW SINGLE MOTHERHOOD IS PERCEIVED

How Your Baby daddy Views you: Of course all relationships vary to some degree but generally speaking, these are three common scenarios which describe how your baby daddy might perceive you: (1) your baby daddy is still into you (2) your baby daddy is not into you but respects you and (3) your baby daddy is not into you and may not even like you.

Scenario 1 is the most favorable situation for a baby momma but is also the most uncommon of the three scenarios. In this scenario, although you and your baby daddy are not together, he still has feelings for you and would like to reconcile. His reaction to your pregnancy was either: (1) he was surprised but elated to learn you were carrying his child or (2) he was elated but not surprised because he was sexually reckless and not opposed to the idea of starting a family with you. He possesses a great deal of respect for you, your life and your goals and he can envision spending his life with you. Furthermore he is still physically attracted to you and is not upset that you had his baby. For whatever reason, you no longer wish to remain in the relationship. You may have started dating again and may feel as though your "Mr. Right" could be someone other than your baby daddy. If your desire is "to get back out there" and see if you can "do better," than your baby daddy, do what you feel you need to do. More likely than not, you may realize, now that you are a mother, the level of sincerity and commitment you are demanding from new men is way too much for them and they are not willing or able to fulfill your needs and act as a stepfather to your child. In most cases, these new prospects are not willing to give this kind of dedication to another man's baby momma. If you are a woman in scenario 1, you should strongly consider trying to make the relationship with your baby daddy work and eventually consider marrying him. If your baby daddy is not abusive or toxic, the best decision you can make for your child, and ultimately yourself, is to become a family. Initially, this may not be easy but your child is worth the effort. The attempt to make this relationship work will require hard work and relationship counseling but is much better than the alternative—continuing to date single people who may not have children and may not understand your lifestyle. So, if your baby daddy is willing to make things work, take him up on this offer before he changes his mind!

As stated earlier, in scenario 2, your baby daddy is not into you but respects you. In a nutshell, your baby daddy views you as a woman who is not suitable to be his wife. In this scenario, your baby daddy had absolutely no intentions of getting you pregnant but is willing to own up to his responsibilities. He believes your life is "together" enough to have a baby with you. He is confident that his child will be safe and adequately provided for when he is absent and he appreciates you for this. Your reliability puts him at ease and allows him reassurance that he can maintain a certain level of freedom to continue to "do him." Although he is happy with you as his baby momma he does not believe you are good enough to be his wife and will continue dating until he finds her. Also, do not be surprised if he no longer finds you sexually attractive. Although this may be how the relationship ensued, as we all know, things change physically after giving birth. If you have not captured a man's heart and developed a connection deeper than a physical attraction, it is not likely he will overlook the changes to your body. This may sound harsh but men are extremely physical and may only overlook these physical changes if they love you unconditionally. When a real man loves you unconditionally, it will be no surprise. He would have already married you or he will begin taking the necessary steps toward making you his wife.

Lastly, Scenario 3 is the worst case scenario. In this scenario your baby daddy is not into you and may not even like you. This is typically the case if your baby daddy suggested having an abortion, denied that the child was his or if he outright refused to be involved in his child's life. His lack of involvement makes it very clear how he feels about you. He may be upset that you disregarded his feelings by having his child against his wishes. Furthermore, he may not be financially capable of taking care of a child. Your decision to have his child despite his inability to provide may leave him feeling emasculated or embarrassed. He may resent you for damaging his self-esteem and his likelihood of becoming a successful man. In this case, your baby daddy may further resent you for imposing on his freedom. He most likely does not love or even like you. Women may find this perplexing but men actually have sex with women they dislike all the time. To men, sex does not constitute love or a relationship. Sex is just sex. This scenario is unfortunate but often too common.

It is important to acknowledge how your baby daddy views you because it will tell you a lot about how you feel about yourself. A child is the most important gift you will ever give a man. The decision to give a man a child who doesn't think highly of you is an indication of tragically low self-worth. It is important to analyze why you believe it is acceptable to give a man something so invaluable if he does not deserve it.

How Your Future Prospects View You: Dating for a baby momma is far more difficult than it is for single women. Also, be sure to keep in mind the double standard present for single mothers when dating that does not necessarily exist for single fathers. Unfortunately, this is one of those double standards that do not work in a woman's favor. Single mothers typically have primary custody which makes their dating lives much more restricted than the fathers who may still live as bachelors. Women need to understand that when they agree to single motherhood, they are agreeing to subject themselves to a greater disadvantage than the father when trying to date. Another disadvantage women may encounter, that their male counterparts will not, is the issue of the "postpartum body." Clearly a man cannot carry a baby and will remain emotionally and physically unscathed. Women on the other hand, may experience emotional trauma such as postpartum depression and often display physical signs of the miracle of childbirth. While a married woman's husband may find these changes admirable, courageous or a beautiful reminder of their child's birth, single men may not share these same sentiments. However, this section is not about the challenges single mothers face when dating. Instead, this section focuses on how single mothers are perceived by men while trying to date. Needless to say, all men are slightly different. So, let's discuss men from different backgrounds and then discuss their different perceptions.

The Top-Notch Man: The top-notch man is the ideal man. He is the cream of the crop, the crème de la crème and total marriage material. He is a highly educated, intellectual, well-rounded, successful man. He is goal oriented, motivated and responsible. He respects women because he had respectful female influences in his upbringing. Similarly, he knows his role and responsibilities as a man because he was raised with strong, positive male influences. He respects his legacy and understands the importance of having a strong woman by his side to further advance his legacy. He likes women who value marriage and family. Romantically he is exclusive and will oppose the idea of having children by any woman other than his wife. He prefers to date women who do not have children because he has none. When dating, he is future-oriented and desires a woman with a clean slate. He wants to build his legacy with his family name and will likely have a hard time taking a woman seriously if she already has a child. Trying to comprehend why she did something as permeant as having a child under such uncertain circumstances, will make him question her judgment and foresight. Because he was raised to be responsible and methodical in planning his life, he expects his partner to display those same qualities. Landing a top-notch man will be tough for a baby momma. In addition to his concerns, she may be met with resistance from his family and friends for her prior indiscretions.

The Average Joe: The average Joe is a regular guy. He is very "middle-of-the-road." He is relatable to most women and has the potential to be a great man. Growing up, he may not have had the best male or female influences but they were adequate enough to give him the foundation necessary to become a good person and a decent man with a lot of potential. He is not necessarily opposed to dating a baby momma and in some cases may be a baby daddy himself. Unlike the top-notch man, a woman having a child won't scare off the average Joe. However, you may find he constantly feels caught in a catch 22 when dating you. Men are quite possessive, so when dating you, his feelings toward your baby daddy may be torn. He will respect you if you've maintained an amicable relationship with your child's father but may eventually feel overwhelmed, annoyed, or turned-off by his constant presence. On the other hand, if you have an estranged or terrible relationship with your child's father, initially the average Joe may feel relieved to not have to compete with another man. Simultaneously, he may question your judgment for having a child with a man who doesn't help you or treats you poorly. He may even lose respect for you knowing your baby daddy doesn't respect you. Another catch 22 the average Joe may experience when dating a baby momma is the conflict concerning how much or how little time you have to spend with him. If a woman is a dedicated single mother who makes her child her main priority, she'll have limited time to dedicate to dating and he can absolutely forget about spontaneous dates or trips. The lack of time the dedicated single mother has for the average Joe may not hold his interest for very long and he might continue to pursue other options. On the other hand if a single mother makes herself, not her child, her main priority and allows as much time as she wants to entertain dates, she may keep the interest of the average Joe, initially. The average Joe may feel as if dating a single mom isn't so bad after all. He is able to see her as much as a woman without children until he realizes she does in fact have a child. This realization may make him question her priorities and values and may lead him to believe she is not a good mother. He might feel guilty for occupying time that should be delegated to her child, which may make him distance himself. Or in the event he meets her child, the parental neglect will be apparent from the child's behavioral problems and this will definitely be the "nail in the coffin" for this relationship.

The Good-For-Nothing Man: The final category and by far the worst type of guy is the good-for-nothing man. This type of man usually has "daddy issues." Because he was not raised with his father or a positive male role model, he is clueless about what it means to be a man. He is a constant let down because he is unaware of his civil responsibility to protect and provide for his woman. He will often hurt or disrespect you unintentionally due to his immaturity and pure ignorance. He does not participate in chivalrous acts such as opening your door or taking you on dates. Subconsciously, his level of respect for women in general is subpar because his mother may have set a poor example of how a woman should conduct herself. She may have exposed him to multiple men throughout his upbringing, constantly placing more importance on her dating life than on her son. As a result of his mother's indiscretions, he has low self-esteem and deeply rooted trust issues with women. On the other hand, even if his mother did not expose him to a revolving door of men, watching his mother tackle the role of both mom and dad will most certainly leave him confused about the role a man should play in a woman's life. The good-for-nothing man has no objection to dating a baby momma or any type of woman, for that matter. He brings very little to the table, so any woman who will give him the time of day is "his type." The good-for-nothing man views single mothers the same way he views all women. He has hang-ups and makes generalizations about all women. Because of this, he categorizes women based on what they can do or provide for him. He believes a good woman will house him, feed him and have sex with him, although he contributes nothing in return besides his dick.

Because of his poor upbringing, the good-for-nothing man is likely to have multiple children by different women because he has no respect for family or legacy. He is desensitized to the broken family structure and is often drawn to single mothers more than the average Joe. So to all baby mommas, beware of the good-for-nothing man. He may seem easy to impress because he is not concerned with how many children you have or how you are raising them because he means you no good. He is not interested in or capable of making you a better woman or mother. He is only interested in taking advantage of you and knowing you are a single mother may make it easy for him to do so. If you encounter the good-for-nothing man, run in the opposite direction! If you are currently dating, housing, feeding, or having sex with the good-for-nothing man, don't deceive yourself into believing you can change him. Because his problems are subconscious and deep rooted issues stemming from his childhood, only a licensed therapist can help him become a real man.

How Society Views You: People are judgmental in general. They will judge you based on your race, religion, gender, etc. So, needless to say, when people see you pregnant or with your child and not wearing a wedding ring they may form an opinion about you. This however does not apply to single mothers who are divorcees. People may view single mothers who are divorcees with a higher regard than a baby momma. Being divorced obviously implies that at one point you were married which means you respect and are capable of a commitment. The divorcee approached motherhood in the correct order but unfortunately the marriage did not work out. People will be sympathetic to a marriage ending but might not lend the same compassion to a woman choosing to have a child without the stability of a committed marriage.

When considering how society views baby mommas, there are common but differing perceptions people assume. These perceptions are influenced by factors such as an individual's upbringing, their personal beliefs, their level of education, their environment and their socioeconomic status. People from different backgrounds hold different viewpoints and can be categorized into the following groups: (1) "respectable and conscious-minded people," (2) "the masses or sheeple" and (3) "low-lives and scum."

"Respectable and conscious-minded people": These informed—and usually educated—individuals may view a baby momma as negligent or immature. They respect a specific order in which life should happen. They believe responsible people make a conscious decision to get married and then have children. The fact that a woman neglected to maintain this order in her life, may make her appear reckless or irresponsible to them. The only truth behind these sentiments is that successful people plan. They have direction and know where they are going. They understand that the decision to have children is so monumental, it requires preparation, resources and support. So, if you have a child before considering these very important elements, you have to wonder if these ideas are in fact true.

"The masses or sheeple": The masses or sheeple are members of society who "go with the flow" and are generally agreeable with the dominate thinking of the majority—regardless of whether it is good or bad, right or wrong. Their perspective on this issue will vary depending upon the general consensus held in their environment or community. They may be somewhat indifferent as to how they view you. They are most likely the "give you the benefit of the doubt" type of people. They may be less critical and might only look down on you if you are a bad mother rather than judge you for simply being a single mother.

"Low-lives and scum": Lastly, "low-lives and scum" may view single mothers in a different way. Low-life men, like parasites, either intentionally or sometimes subconsciously seek out single mothers who appear vulnerable or abandoned. They target women who are susceptible to being taken advantage of or preyed upon and this is exactly what they will do. If they can sense that a single mother is desperate or has low self-esteem, they will present themselves as a savor or a knight in shining armor, only to further exploit her current situation. They are the type of "men" that will experience no indignity when moving in with a single mother without contributing financially and may even take advantage of other resources like her EBT. Low-life women will identify with your situation and will reassure you that your misfortunes are not a result of your choices, but are in fact attributable to "some selfish man." For these women the saying "misery loves company" rings true. They will often engage in pointless baby daddy bashing sessions that are counterproductive to your growth. They do not want you to see the error of your ways because if you accept accountability for your mistakes, they too will have to reevaluate their choices.

At the end of the day, the most important aspect of your life's journey is your character and what you contribute to society—not what others think of you. However, it is important to be aware of and understand these perceptions before you have children and if you are already a single mother. Acknowledging these perceptions do not necessarily make them correct but understand, at some point they may have an impact on your life. The idea is not to place a great deal of emphasis on being accepted by others. The idea is to ensure your choices reflect who you are and how you want to be perceived. Realize, many of your choices, including how you structure your family, may only be relatable or acceptable to a specific class of people. So, consider the different viewpoints of "respectable and conscious-minded people," "the masses or sheeple" and "low-lives and scum." Understand that your life choices will make you more relatable to certain demographics and perspectives. "Respectable and conscious-minded people" and "low-lives and scum" share completely different viewpoints on the proper way to structure a family. Depending on how your family is structured, you may find it easier to coexist with people who relate to your choices and are not offended by your lifestyle. Different groups of people have different levels of discipline and different standards for what is and isn't acceptable. "Respectable and conscious-minded people" have high standards for their conduct while "low-lives and scum" have low standards and find most behaviors acceptable. So before you start your family, consider what type of environment and what type of people you want influencing your children's mindset.

Make sure your life choices and how you structure your family is in alignment with your desired position in society. For instance, if you want to be successful, with successful friends and neighbors, make sure you thoughtfully plan out your success. Success does not happen by chance. It is a premeditated and formulated sequence of choices and results. Similarly, building a successful family is also a premeditated and formulated plan that usually begins with a successful marriage. This idea has been proven over and over and over again by successful people. So if you choose not to construct your family this way, your actions might imply that you do not care about yourself, your future or your children's future or that you are simply naive and foolish and are unaware to what extent you are not ready to be a parent. This may sound harsh, but it is time for black women to redefine "what is normal" for us. We must raise our standards for ourselves and fully understand that taking control of how we are perceived should be important to us as queens. If you are a woman who does not have children, consider these societal perceptions prior to deciding how you want to have children and think long and hard about what you want their legacy to be.

KEEPING YOUR CROWN

THE EFFECTS ON YOUR CHILD

Aside from how society may perceive you as a baby momma, the single most important factor to consider is how raising a child outside of marriage will affect your child. It is imperative to be aware of the harmful psychological effects your child may experience as a result of not being raised in a stable, two-parent household. When having a child outside of marriage your child will experience one of three scenarios: (1) The present father who co-parents with you (2) The inconsistent father who is in and out of your child's life and (3) The absent father who has no involvement in raising your child.

The Present Father: The present father is actively involved in your child's life. Your child knows and loves him as his or her father. They understand the co-parenting schedule and are accustomed to spending time separately with both parents. This situation is a bit more stable for the child than the other two scenarios but may later influence how the child structures his or her own relationships in the future. The child may likely have a case of "commitment confusion" and "procreation recklessness." "Commitment confusion" suggests that because the child has not witnessed both parents functioning together, under the same roof, raising the child with common goals and a combined parenting plan, the child may be oblivious to the amount of compromise and sacrifice required to build a successful, loving and lasting relationship. They may misunderstand what a healthy relationship and marriage entails. It is crucial that children witness their parents display love and respect within a relationship. It is also crucial that they witness a partnership in which each parent shares part of the responsibilities to make the family function. Their parents' relationship will be the most influential example of how two people should treat each other. If a child doesn't witness a healthy marriage in the home, they will struggle to fulfill their duties as a committed partner. "Procreation recklessness" suggests that the child may not object to having children with someone they do not see a permanent future with. They may behave sexually irresponsible because they do not find the idea of creating a life within a temporary relationship devastating, considering they find normalcy in being raised in a broken home. Because they have witnessed their parents raising them separately, they may not value the beauty, unity and solidarity that a good marriage provides. They may not understand what a true commitment looks like. When the time comes for him or her to have children of their own, they may mirror your choices. They too will likely end up becoming a "present baby momma" or a "present baby daddy" because they are not marriage oriented. They won't fantasize about marriage because this was not the example presented for them. We've all heard the expression "you can't miss what you've never had." So, if a child has never witnessed the many benefits that come with being raised by a unified partnership, the child won't understand how disadvantageous it is to be raised without one. The truth is, children do what you do, not what you say. "Marriage comes first" is not a concept that was instilled in them and as a result they may not weigh the decision to have children as heavy as they should. They may not consciously seek out their life partner before starting a family and instead may procreate with someone they don't see a future with. This is a dangerous problem because as an adult, like you, your child may perpetuate the vicious cycle of creating broken homes that is destroying the black community.

The Inconsistent Father: The inconsistent father pops in and out of your child's life. He has a tendency to make plans with your child but is often a no-show. One year he'll show up to your child's birthday party with gifts galore and the next year he won't even call. His unpredictability will surely send your child on an emotional rollercoaster. Unfortunately, children tend to internalize their feelings of abandonment because they are not yet mature enough to understand why their father is so inconsistent. They think it is somehow their fault that their father doesn't want to spend more time with them and may begin to feel unimportant. A child's development relies heavily on having consistency and structure. As a result of experiencing these inconsistencies, your child may develop a fragile self-esteem and trust issues which may later affect how your child will operate in future relationships. Their overall standards and expectations for what constitutes a healthy relationship in the future might be extremely low. Because they are used to disappointment and being let down, the child (especially girls) might tolerate inconsistent behavior from their future partners. Eventually they may make excuses for and even justify their partner's actions. If the child is sensitive and emotionally scarred, their trust issues might prevent them from letting their guard down in an attempt to avoid further disappointment. They may loath the vulnerability required to develop a sincere connection and as a result may forgo meaningful relationships. Once again your child will, more likely than not, mirror the behavior they witnessed from you. Your daughter may view an inconsistent man as a suitable father for her children. She may find little fault in his inconsistent behavior because this is all she knows. She may not put up too much of a fight and may have little opposition to his lack of involvement. Because she does not understand the full scope of a father's responsibilities, she might over-praise the little things he does and the little time he spends as if it were adequate. She may constantly sell herself short in this respect and in turn, might expose her children to the same disservice she experienced while growing up. Your son, on the other hand, may not fear having children because he does not perceive fatherhood as challenging, time consuming or as a large responsibility. Because his father was not fully invested, he may not believe being a father is a full-time responsibility. To him it's more like a part-time hobby or activity and he may not feel terrified or overwhelmed at the idea of having a child. Eventually he too, may become an "inconsistent baby daddy."

The Absent Father: The absent father's role in your child's life is self-explanatory. He is nowhere to be found. For varying reasons the absent father either chose not to participate, or you felt it was best to not involve him in raising his child. The child may or may not have been introduced to their father at some point but he has no involvement in his child's life. Not only is the biological father not present in this scenario, no other man is consistently present to serve as a positive male father figure. Of the three scenarios, this is the most hurtful and damaging to your child. It is very difficult for a child to conceptualize why their father completely "bailed on them." At this point their father becomes a figment of the child's imagination and they sadly fantasize about having a relationship with him. The need for a father or father figure can become so intense that the child will be happy if any man fills this void.

This void or "daddy issues" can cause a world of pain, desperation and confusion. The child may once again blame themselves or even blame you for their father's absence. This is a frustrating situation for a child and can cause them to act out in unfavorable ways. Like the child with the inconsistent father, children with absent fathers typically suffer from self-esteem issues but on a greater level. Although the inconsistent father is in and out of the child's life, when he is present, he might profess his love for his child. While his actions are inconsistent with his words, he may occasionally tell his child he loves them. However, the child with the absent father may never hear their father express his love. This is incredibly painful to a child. Feeling as though one parent did not care enough to stick around, may make a child feel discarded, unloved, and unworthy.

In addition to experiencing overwhelming emotional strife, children who are products of a single-mother-household with an absent father are often severely neglected. They primarily may experience neglect in one of two scenarios: (1) The over-worked single mother who forfeits spending time with her child to provide adequate resources and (2) The single mother who receives government assistance which allows her to spend more time at home, but forfeits adequate resources.

Scenario 1 (The Working/Over-Worked Single Mother): In scenario 1, the child lives in a safe neighborhood and attends a good or decent school. This child has most of his or her essential needs met such as a clean home with his or her own bedroom, adequate meals, appropriate clothes, transportation etc. These essentials are afforded to the child because his or her mother may work multiple jobs or countless hours at one job to make this standard of living possible. According to the 2013 U.S. Census Bureau, the median income for households led by single mothers is only $26,000 a year, compared with $84,000 for married couples. So, in order for most single mothers to provide adequate resources, one can imagine the amount of time she must commit to her job. However, in this scenario, the child may experience neglect in terms of time spent and in child rearing. Having quality time with their parents is essential to a child's development. Quality time is a major way for children to satiate their need for attention. It makes them feel valued, validated and loved. If this need is unfulfilled, you may witness the child behave poorly and display attention seeking behavior to compensate for the lack of attention at home. In order for a child to become well-rounded and fully developed, they need individualized attention from two parents. A child with an absent father is already at a disadvantage. So, having a single mother who is constantly working may eliminate adequate parental influence from the child's life altogether.

As previously mentioned, the second way in which the over-worked single mother might neglect her child is through inadequate child rearing. Child rearing consists of teaching your child manners, etiquette, social skills, and the difference between right and wrong. Instilling these values and principles in a child requires time and constant effort. A parent who lacks time may forgo teaching their child many of these essential principles which will impact the child's behavior. For instance, the child may become unmanageable and begin displaying behavior many describe as "having no home training." Although the over-worked single mother has more resources to offer her child, she must understand that investing too little time may be detrimental to the child.

It is also important to mention that young boys growing up in this environment may be impacted in a different way. Witnessing their mother fill the role as the sole provider for the family, coupled with not having any male influence, may make for an extremely delicate boy who may later become confused about his role and responsibilities as man. This serves as a disclaimer to single mothers raising their sons without a father figure or male influence present; women will never be capable of raising a man. No amount of resources she provides will compensate for not having his father's involvement, nor can she buy him the tools he needs to become a real man. Raising strong black men is essential to creating thriving black communities. Being raised without a father figure and instead by a single mother trying to fulfill both roles, is essentially handicapping our young boys and preventing them from becoming powerful assets in our community.

Scenario 2 (The Single Mother who Receives Government Assistance): In Scenario 2, the single mother who receives government assistance but forfeits comfort and adequate resources, provides her child with a different set of circumstances. In most cases, women who receive government aid live in low-income areas. According to the 2013 U.S. Census Bureau, households led by single mothers are five times more likely to live in poverty than married couples. Of those families living in poverty, 51.9% live in "extreme poverty" meaning their incomes are below half of the federal poverty level and are making less than $9,900 a year. Many of their neighbors are also single mothers with a similar set of circumstances. Consequently, the community may primarily be comprised of countless children and a disproportionate amount of adults to supervise them. According to the 2015 U.S. Census Bureau, families with only one parent present are much less likely to supervise and control their teenage children. The number of unsupervised children in the community, often leads to rambunctious behavior and can eventually escalate into neighborhood crime. Again, the 2015 U.S. Census Bureau indicates that low-class youth commit four times more violent crimes than middle-class youth. So, unfortunately at some point, the child may have exposure to or even contribute to unscrupulous activity within the potentially crime-infested community.

Along with these negative external influences, the child's home life may not be much better. The child may not have adequate space, especially if the family is confined to a housing project or an apartment community. Even if the family occupies a larger, subsidized-home (or something similar), these properties are typically unkept. Because the tenants who occupy these homes do not own them, they may lack a sense of pride in ownership. They did not purchase the home and thus do not view it as an investment that needs to be protected. There is no incentive to maintain the home properly nor are they concerned with property value or a sense of community. Additionally, the school systems in low-income areas are underfunded and neglected. The lack of a sufficient education combined with the depressing hopelessness present in impoverished communities can adversely impact other areas of life. Everything from their health, diet and physical upkeep may be affected as well.

For example, even if the family receives food stamps, they may not have an adequate understanding of nutrition to use the resource most effectively. Aside from their everyday discomforts, the inability to afford common luxuries such as transportation and appropriate clothes will further lessen their overall quality of life.

The stressors associated with low-income living and poverty are mentally and emotionally overwhelming for anyone, not to mention a single mother who's lacking support. So, although the mother may be present in the home and not working 40+ hours a week, it is not safe to say that she will be mentally and emotionally available to her child. In this scenario, the child may experience a "lose-lose" situation considering they are being denied both adequate resources and time spent with their parent. Not to mention, a single parent under such constant stress may be incapable of providing adequate supervision. This is a serious concern when combined with the dangers of such neighborhoods. Children in these environments are often overexposed to sex, drugs and crime and cannot afford to be neglected. They may come face to face with intense and life altering, adult situations they are ill-equipped to navigate successfully. The last thing a parent would want is for their child to find themselves in an irreversible situation such as teen pregnancy or being imprisoned before they can even rationalize their choices.

Regardless of whether a child is being raised by the over-worked single mother or the single mother who receives government assistance, all children will greatly suffer when being raised without a father or a consistent father figure. Because having an absent father is so damaging to children, it is important to discuss individually, how girls and boys will be affected by their father's lack of involvement. The old saying rings true that a child's relationship with their opposite sex parent, greatly influences how the child will interact with the opposite sex in the future and will ultimately influence what type of partner they will choose.

How Having an Absent Father Affects Girls in Scenario 2: It is imperative that a woman understands what role a man should play in her life. It is her father's responsibility to be the first man to demonstrate chivalrous behavior. Her father is responsible for establishing a benchmark for the level of kindness, generosity and respect she should expect from men. He is supposed to protect and provide for the family. If this is the example a father provides for his daughter, she will expect nothing less from men she encounters in the future. If a poor example is set or if no example is established at all, young girls become very damaged and confused. The majority of young girls with "daddy issues" will also suffer from low self-esteem and low self-worth. Once again, these feelings of abandonment often leave children questioning their value and importance. These self-esteem issues may become a major problem for the young girl as she begins dating. Because of her father's absence, she may seek validation, acceptance and attention from men. Her father's absence will cause her to feel unworthy and she may subconsciously desire approval from men to feel worthy or good enough. In addition to needing acceptance from men, she may also lack the ability to distinguish between a good man and a bad man. She has no point of reference, demands, or expectations for how a man should treat her because her father was not present to establish these protocols. This lack of understanding can cause a world of trouble. Young women place a great deal of importance on their love lives and relationships and can unknowingly involve themselves in toxic relationships that can completely derail their lives. If, in the midst of her naivety, she falls for a man who is dishonest, manipulative or abusive she may lack the integrity or confidence needed to turn him away. A confused young woman with such large emotional voids may even fight for the love of a man who doesn't understand how to love her properly. Early introductions to these types of abusive relationships can set a tone or establish a dysfunctional norm for her dating life. In the event she is involved in an abusive relationship, the situation can continue to escalate because there is no father or father figure present to protect her and reprimand the abuser. According to the 2015 U.S. Census Bureau, a one-parent household headed by a female is more vulnerable to criminal attacks. Protection is one integral benefit of having a man present that single mothers often overlook or undervalue until it is far too late.

    Another serious disadvantage for young girls dealing with "daddy issues" and self-esteem problems will surface as she becomes sexually active. Her desperate need for attention from men may be used against her to exploit her sexually. Young girls with "daddy issues" are often extremely promiscuous. They may often confuse casual sex with love and may frequently engage in sexual activity to fill the void created by her father's absence. Again, because they lack protection, these girls are often the victims of sexual abuse and molestation. When a young girl is exploited or sexualized to this degree, she may form a dysfunctional relationship with sex. Her sexuality may become, in her mind, her only source of power or control. These confused ideals about sex, combined with the financial difficulties common in single parent households often leads young girls down the path to involvement in the sex industry. It is not uncommon for young girls with "daddy issues" in a bad environment, with a lack of supervision and a lack of resources to become strippers or far worse. It is also not uncommon for girls growing up under these circumstances to become young, single mothers themselves. According to the Center for Disease Control's Division of Reproductive Health, teen pregnancy is often cyclical, meaning; girls born from teen mothers are likely to become teen mothers themselves. Women under these circumstances typically perpetuate the lifestyle their single mother provided for them, thus turning this mistake into a devastating generational problem. There will be a few extraordinary exceptions in which the child's upbringing is so devastating, he or she courageously makes completely different life choices to escape this cycle but unfortunately this scenario is not common enough.

How Having an Absent Father Affects Boys in Scenario 2: As mentioned earlier, single mothers who receive assistance to provide for their children often live in less than desirable neighborhoods, with inadequate school systems. Again, because of environmental stress the single mother is tackling alone, she may not have the mental capacity to supervise her child properly. Young boys growing up under these circumstances will desperately crave male influence. As one can imagine, this is not the easiest environment to navigate. Men rely heavily on other male perspectives and support when learning how to survive in the streets. Because many of the young men in these neighborhoods are lacking a positive male role model at home, they tend to be drawn to older men in the neighborhood for guidance. In some cases this can be positive because let's face it, having a male role model is better than not having one. Unfortunately, many of the men in the neighborhood may not be the best influences. Considering the circumstances in these neighborhoods are so desperate and hopeless, the older male influence usually entails, teaching young boys how to survive by any means necessary. Coupled with inadequate school systems and limited job opportunities, these boys are left with few options other than involvement with illegal activities such as selling drugs and armed robbery. Although these young boys feel they are becoming men by learning how to survive in the streets, in reality, the activities they are engaging in will leave them with limited options—usually resulting in death or prison. Statistics reveal that 1 in 3 black men will become incarcerated at some point in their lives. According to *Prison and the Poverty Trap*, an article published in *The New York Times* by John Tierney in 2013, "for black men in their 20's and early 30's, without a high school diploma, the incarceration rate is so high—nearly 40 percent nationwide—that they're more likely to be behind bars than to have a job."

There is no question that black men are being systematically targeted by institutions that profit from the mass incarceration of black men and the free labor they provide while imprisoned. These private institutions are generating enormous profits by housing mostly black and Hispanic inmates. This racist and corrupt business model is effectively eliminating the black male population—especially in low-income areas—leaving these communities debilitated, powerless and in a state of dependency. Needless to say, there is nothing black men can do for their women, families or their communities from behind bars or in the ground. With this harsh reality in mind, women must understand that when raising black boys in such hopeless environments, without any positive male influence, single mothers are basically aiding in the systematic destruction of black men and black communities. Black women must stop having children out of wedlock and in low-income areas because the risk is simply too high. It is urgent that single mothers stop perpetuating this cycle of broken homes and start understanding the magnitude of their choices and how their role can aid in the destruction of our communities.

KEEPING YOUR CROWN

HOW "DADDY ISSUES" ARE DESTROYING "BLACK LOVE"

In addition to the previously mentioned harmful effects children endure, single parent households are also threatening the institution of marriage and productive, loving relationships. When women have children without the example of marriage, they are contributing to a generation of people who do not know how to love each other. There's an influx of children being raised without fathers and suffering from daddy issues. These children grow into adults who have no clue how to love another person. They unceasingly struggle to form loving partnerships. Because positive examples of "black love" are rarely demonstrated in the home, our young kings and queens do not know how to treat each other properly. People gripe and complain about the lack of love in society nowadays. This lack of love and respect for one another is apparent in today's music. The lyrics in music are a clear indication that the majority of our youth do not know how to perform respectful exchanges while dating. They insist they want "that 90's R&B love." Well, that love dissipated when people began having children out of wedlock at alarming rates. The newer generations are not witnessing "black love" like the older generations. In many instances, their parents don't even like each other and fail to co-parent respectfully. What can children born from these loveless relationships possibly know about love? Broken homes are making people lonelier than ever. Even when children are produced from loving, healthy marriages, they cannot form healthy connections with people with daddy issues. These dysfunctions are too overwhelming for stable people to repair or tolerate. Relationships are built on trust and people who suffer from daddy issues are often too distrusting—due to abandonment issues and other let downs—to give and receive love properly. Human beings are intensely interconnected and need positive human interaction to be happy. People fail to realize how the mistakes they make when "raising" their children will affect how their children will connect to and interact with other people. In order for your children to give and receive love, they must first witness a healthy, functioning relationship from their mother and father. As a result of witnessing dysfunctional relationships and in turn, developing daddy issues, women are more promiscuous and men are more feminine than ever before! This role-reversal is out of control and must be stopped. Without the opportunity to watch their parents function in a successful relationship, our youth will continue to be confused about gender roles and what responsibilities they are expected to fulfill as men and women. Not only is the single motherhood epidemic ruining black communities, it is also destroying "black love." This problem must be combated to enrich and improve the state of Black America.

Another problem with the single motherhood epidemic is that it creates disrespectful and strained relationships between black men and women. Black men and women must treat each other better and strive for loving, healthy and respectful relationships. It is malicious and selfish to force a man to become a father if he is not ready and if he is financially incapable. Forcing a man to become a father prematurely is damaging to his manhood, his self-worth and lessens his likelihood of succeeding. Black women must stop pinning children on underdeveloped black men before they are established and capable of providing for a child. Sure it may seem as though women are receiving more blame and liability in this situation but this is simply because women are typically more mature. Women also have control over what happens to their bodies. Women can use birth control, require men to wear condoms and use a morning after pill following a reckless night. She can even terminate an accidental pregnancy conceived with an immature man who will undoubtedly be an unfit father. It is ultimately the woman's decision that determines whether she becomes a mother and whether he becomes a father. Part of being a queen entails assuming the role of a protector over our black kings. Don't make decisions that will negatively impact a black man's life if you have the power to avoid doing so. Don't take advantage of a man's naivety and stupidity by forcing him to fill a role he is incapable of fulfilling. Black women must protect black men in situations when they don't know any better. If we expect men to protect us physically, we must protect them judiciously by keeping their best interests in mind, especially when it benefits the black community. Additionally, black men are wrongly incarcerated everyday so don't allow child support jail time to serve as another means of incarcerating black men. Black women must stop procreating with broke men, expecting them to furnish loads of money once the child arrives, as if his financial situation would have miraculously improved overnight. The decision to become a parent signifies that one is mature enough to "bite the bullet" and accept the consequences that come along with having a child. When a woman chooses to have a child by a man who lacks resources, this decision indicates that she is content with a life of financial hardship. Don't penalize a man for being a loser after you've allowed him to get you pregnant. At this point, you are the one to blame for turning a "little boy" into a father instead of denying him time, attention, energy and sex as a real woman should. Instead, black men and women must support one another in becoming successful. Black men and women must love each other better. We must agree to wear protection and focus on becoming better people prior to becoming parents. Having children out of wedlock and prior to achieving success is damaging to both black men and women as well as to our children and our community.

REMEMBER, YOUR CHILD IS NOT YOUR FRIEND

Another dysfunction that may arise as a result of being raised by a single mother is the development of a codependent or inappropriate relationship between the child and their mother. If the child and their mother form a habit of relying on one another for support, the dynamic of their relationship may suffer. Without a father or father figure present, some mothers may unintentionally misuse or misunderstand the role she is to play in her child's life. This inappropriate relationship typically plays out in one of two ways: (1) The single mother who thinks her daughter is her best friend and (2) The single mother who treats her son like he is her "man."

In the first instance, as a result of being a young mother, having limited social interactions or after being abandoned by the child's father, the single mother may latch onto her daughter, viewing her as her only support system. This single mother designates her daughter as her best friend and confidante, adopting an "all we have is each other" philosophy. To avoid feeling lonely, she confides in her daughter and establishes a relationship only another grown woman should occupy in her life. She tells her daughter about the ups and downs of her day. She gossips with her child about neighbors, coworkers and her crushes. She may even listen to the same music as her daughter and watch the same television programs, which further blurs the boundary lines and leaves an implication that she and her daughter are peers. This behavior is inappropriate and should not occur between a mother and her child. According to *Why You Can't Be Your Child's Friend*, an article by Janet Lehman published on EmpoweringParents.com, confiding too much in your child relinquishes a great deal of your control as a parent. "You're not in charge anymore, and they [your children] may feel like they're responsible for your emotions in some way. But this isn't fair to kids—they are not meant to play that role with us. As they grow up, they really need to learn what their place is in the world, and we need to give them time to grow into each phase. Treating them like a peer doesn't allow them to just be kids in the long run."

When you overshare too much of your business with your daughter, you appear vulnerable to her. As a result of oversharing, she will feel an obligation to protect you and be there for you. However, this is not your daughter's responsibility in your life. We all face complications throughout our day-to-day lives but it is inappropriate to share this information with your child. To ensure your child feels complacent and at ease, do not concern them with adult issues. Instead of confiding in your daughter, you need to be there for her. Your job is to ensure she feels secure and stable. You should not attempt to derive security or validation from her. Do not take her childhood away because you rely on her "friendship" for your own comfortability. Allow your daughter to find suitable friendships among her actual peers at school. She needs to have your guidance and leadership, not your friendship or companionship.

The second instance occurs when a single mother treats her son as though he is her "man." Because a man is not present in the home, this single mother believes if she overpraises her son, he will somehow understand what it means to be a man. She believes by calling him a "king" and by telling him he is "the man of the house," he will eventually conceptualize what it actually means to become a protector and a provider. She also deceives herself into believing that overindulging in affection such as kissing him on the lips and allowing him to sleep in her bed is an appropriate remedy to compensate for his father's absence. Unfortunately this behavior has harmful adverse effects.

KEEPING YOUR CROWN

Little boys do not need to be pampered or coddled. By being overly affectionate with her son, this single mother is actually making her son extremely soft. According to *Are Black Mothers Failing to Raise their Sons* by L. Nicole Williams, an article on Madamenoire.com, "it is that mama's boy inclination that fosters irresponsibility, unaccountability and laziness. It is what creates the imbalance in households minus dad and ultimately stunts the developmental process." Furthermore, once he reaches adulthood, he may be confused about how a woman should treat him and what she is expected to do for him. Although he may lack many qualities necessary to be considered a good man, he will expect women to go above and beyond for him like his mother did. A bigger problem can arise if his mother continues this behavior once he begins dating. Her possessive and overprotective behavior will be problematic for women who express interest in him. These boys will earn the title of a "momma's boy" and may find intense opposition from women while dating if he and his mother continue this codependent, dysfunctional relationship.

Both types of inappropriate relationships are damaging to a child's development. Children need structure, boundaries and discipline to grow into responsible and decent adults. Children need rules and must learn the difference between right and wrong. We have all encountered a mother who insists her kids are her "best friends!" This way of thinking is terribly inappropriate and is not conducive to a child's development. If you cross this boundary and enter into a friendship with your child, this insinuates you and your child are on the same authoritative level. This is dangerous because your child will not only lose respect for you as an authority but he or she will also become confused about how to give the proper respect to other adults. Your job as a parent is to be a leader, a role model, and an authority figure, not a friend. Your child needs your guidance to learn how to navigate life successfully. Children feel safe and stable when boundaries and limitations are set for their behavior. When they make mistakes, they need to be reprimanded to understand the lesson within their mistakes. These teachable moments are necessary for your child to grow into a responsible and productive adult. A child cannot learn these lessons if you take a stance as his or her friend as opposed to an authority figure.

If you realize you have created an inappropriate relationship with your son or daughter, you must immediately change the dynamic of your relationship. You must reestablish yourself as the authority figure in your relationship. You must set boundaries for what topics of conversation are appropriate to discuss with your child. You must reassess what behaviors and activities are appropriate to engage in with your child. Make sure your son or daughter is no longer included in your emotional battles or decision making. Make a concerted effort to be the parent and the authority figure to ensure your son or daughter can enjoy a normal childhood.

HOW YOUR DECISION TO DATE AFFECTS YOUR CHILD

It is unrealistic to expect single mothers to refrain from dating until their child reaches adulthood, however it is important to understand how doing so will affect your child.

KEEPING YOUR CROWN

It is also important to understand that there is a way to date while also protecting your child's best interests. One behavior that should not take place is the "revolving door" of different men coming in and out of your child's life. For children, consistency and stability are essential. Being introduced to even two or three different men is overwhelming and confusing for a child. For the child, this pattern of gaining familiarity with a man who eventually leaves when the relationships ends is damaging and hurtful. If your child develops affection for your boyfriend and things do not work out, once again your child feels abandoned and discarded all over again. This type of repeated behavior will certainly intensify your child's abandonment issues. If the "revolving door" of men happens too frequently, it may cause specific, negative effects on girls and boys individually.

Boys who witness different men in and out of the home often develop a subconscious distrust of women in their adult life. A boy's mother will always be the most highly regarded woman in his life. Because the example his mother provided for him was not monogamous or consistent, he may later distrust a woman's ability to commit to him. Girls on the other hand will be impacted in a different way. Girls are much more complex and can respond to the "revolving door" in a number of ways. As a result of watching her mother place too much emphasis on dating, many young girls will overvalue men and relationships. Rather than placing the proper value on more important objectives like her education, her goals and herself, she may mimic this learned behavior and find it acceptable to "serial date" and over-invest in men. Or she might be so turned off by her mother's choices she becomes skeptical and apprehensive about dating altogether. It gives young girls a dysfunctional outlook on dating and relationships. Ultimately, as a mother, it is your responsibility to avoid introducing people you date to your child until the relationship is serious enough that marriage is the next step. Unless you become engaged or marriage is discussed, it is reckless to continue introducing your boyfriends to your child. If your child's father is not present, it is desirable to have a positive male influence attempt to fill the role of a father-figure in your child's life. However, make sure you only introduce your child to "Mr.

Right" and avoid introducing your child to "Mr. Right Now" over and over and over again.

THE SINGLE EXCEPTION TO SINGLE MOTHERHOOD

It is clear that the optimal way to start a family is with the foundation of a loving marriage. Children greatly benefit when being raised in a stable, nurturing, two-parent household. If a child somehow had the authority to choose how he or she would prefer to be raised, they would undoubtedly choose two mature, married, loving parents. This type of family structure is not only beneficial to the child but is also the foundation needed to create strong and sustainable black communities. However, we do not live in a perfect world and although it is best for children to be afforded two parents, there is one exception in which raising a child outside of the traditional structure can still produce successful children who can still become assets to our community.

This exception applies to the unwed, successful and mature woman who strongly desires to be a mother. In this case, if a woman is highly successful with abundant resources to offer a child, with the proper planning she can negotiate motherhood successfully. Taking into consideration all women have a "biological clock" they are working against, not having a husband shouldn't necessarily stop these capable women from having a baby. It is clear that if a woman of such status decides to have a child, she can avoid the adversities the overworked and assisted-living single mothers face. Her child would be well provided for and allowed all the essential necessities to ensure she raises a well-mannered, confident, educated and ambitious individual.

However, women in this situation are encouraged to not ignore or underestimate the consequences of an absent father figure. Although her level of success makes her a wonderful role model for her child, she must ensure that a positive male influence is consistently present. It is important that the child's father agrees to participate in raising the child prior to making this arrangement. If she decides to use a donor, she must make it a priority to have a brother, uncle or some form of a "father figure" agree to partake in raising her child, prior to making this decision. Having a predetermined male presence or male role model is a must. It is crucial for young boys and girls to have this influential figure in their lives to assist in their development. It is also important to ensure that the male influence in your child's life is committed to delegating time to spend with your child. This is a huge commitment, considering it requires spending time consistently, attending school functions, holidays, birthdays, games, graduations, etc. The idea is to ensure that your child experiences the benefits of having a father figure. Considering all other developmental factors are in place, like a loving home, resources, and positive role models, a child can be raised with the intellect and maturity to understand their mother's decision to have a child outside of marriage. However, children will always have a connection to their biological father and may become curious about "how they got here." So be prepared to answer any paternity questions they may have if the participating father is not the biological father. Additionally, women in this position tend to be more mature in terms of their priorities and are less likely to be distracted by men or dating while raising their children, which can alleviate much of the confusion children born to younger single mothers endure. Simply put, if a woman is in her late 30's or in her 40's and is beyond financially secure and completely ready to be a mother, she should do so. At this point, continuing to wait for a husband is no longer biologically practical. With the proper planning and committed involvement of a father or father figure, it is likely that this arrangement will produce flourishing and happy children.

Black women are becoming single mothers at an alarming rate. After reviewing how damaging this cycle is to our community, black women must stop and ask themselves "why are we doing this?" Statistics reveal how often children from single parent households are living substandard lives and are sometimes even living in poverty. They are receiving more lessons from the "school of hard knocks" than they are from their despairing school systems. This realization alone should make black women think twice before deciding to contribute to this generational catastrophe. The decision to become a mother is one of the most important choices a woman will ever make and black women must give this decision the careful deliberation it deserves. Black women must begin loving themselves and treating themselves like the queens they truly are. We must treat ourselves better and raise our standards for what is and isn't acceptable for our lives. We must demand more for ourselves because we are capable of much more than we are displaying. We must eradicate the idea that being a "strong single mother who don't need no man" is praise-worthy and understand that by doing so we are actually victimizing ourselves and hurting our children and our community. For the black women who currently do not have children, make sure you understand and abide by these principles before starting your family:

1. **Having children is a luxury and is NOT mandatory:** Although many people have children frivolously, the fact remains, being a parent is a huge, continuous responsibility that should only be attempted by prepared, loving parents with stability and adequate resources. If you cannot offer a child absolutely every resource that child needs to be a happy and productive member of society, wait until

you acquire this stability. It is selfish, immature, and destructive to have a child you are incapable of preparing for success. This is especially imperative for women living in low income or impoverished areas. It is a huge injustice to bring a child into poverty. At birth, the cards are already stacked against the child and the probability of him or her becoming a successful, productive member of society is disturbingly low. If you are a woman living under these circumstances, you must make removing yourself from this environment your life's mission! Focus on your studies and do whatever you have to do to attend college elsewhere. Make sure you obtain a college prep high school diploma, take practice SAT courses to improve your SAT score, apply for FAFSA (Free Application for Federal Student Aid) and apply for scholarships. Government assistance, such as Pell Grant and work study programs are available for students who need funding for college tuition. In addition to government grants and academic scholarships, athletic scholarships are another way for students to obtain assistance to afford tuition. Involvement in sports is another viable way to fund your education. Young girls should take advantage of every avenue that will make attending college a possibility. Another viable option for a young woman living in poverty is to join a branch of the military. Enlistment in the military can provide endless opportunities. These careers are respectable and provide stability, discipline, top-notch health benefits, free education and the opportunity to travel the world. There is always a way to improve your circumstances if you are willing to work hard to advance your life. Being poor obviously does not take away a woman's right to have a child but children deserve to be raised in an environment that is safe and conducive to their success. Having children is a luxury and is not mandatory! If you are not in a position to provide a child with a pleasant, comfortable and enjoyable life, do not become a mother until you are able. Fix your current situation before bringing a child into your mess. Being a woman does not make you worthy of being a mother. Being a respectable, responsible, mature wife with adequate resources and a safe and comfortable environment makes you worthy of motherhood. Acquire this level of stability before you have a child to avoid diminishing your child's chances of succeeding. Black America can no longer afford to raise unsuccessful children. When statistics are such that 1 in 3 black men will serve time in prison, we have to eliminate relaxed attitudes about motherhood. Black women must understand and adopt the ideology that every generation must be more successful than the previous generation. If you are not capable of providing a higher standard of living for your child, do not have one.

2. **Children MUST be planned:** Having a child is so important that it requires and most certainly deserves a plan. Babies do not ask to be here and deserve more thought than to be arbitrarily conceived by someone who isn't taking their own life seriously. It is a shame that people will put more thought into planning a vacation than they will into having a child. Don't be one of those foolish

people. If you fail to plan, you plan to fail and a child does not deserve to suffer the consequences of your improper planning. When people don't plan their children or place the proper emphasis on raising them, they make thoughtless mistakes that later create trauma, hang-ups and emotional issues that the child will struggle with in adulthood. We have all heard the expression, "people spend most of their adult life trying to recover from their childhood." This is a tragic reality but is more common than most of us would like to admit. People need to understand they are actually raising a person and must exert more effort into giving "this person" the tools they need to become stable and kind. Many of the adults you dislike or you feel have "bad personalities," were raised by a parent or parents with the same "good" intentions as you. Unfortunately "good intentions" don't create good people. Intentional parenting and planning are more reliable methods of raising good people. Although babies are cute, the "baby phase" is short lived. The amount of work required to mold a baby into a decent human being grows incrementally as the child grows. Being a good parent is a selfless act that requires continuous hard work. People generally share the sentiment that "babies are blessings" but more importantly, would you be a blessing to your baby? You must aim to be the type of parent that your child will consider a blessing once they are old enough to judge the life experience you gave them. With this in mind, treat their life with love, purpose and respect before they even get here.

3. **Get married FIRST:** The one acceptable exception was previously discussed but for all other women, wait until after you are married to have a baby. You can only guarantee that a man is committed to sharing a future with you if he has made you his wife. Then and only then should you give him the honor of having his children. It is important to analyze the male psyche to help you further understand why you should not want to be a man's baby momma. As mentioned earlier, a woman cannot coerce a man into doing something he does

not want to do. Having his child will not make him change the way he feels about you. According to *8 Big Mistakes Baby Mothers Often Make*, an article by L. Nicole Williams on Madamenoire.com "It is very possible for him to love the child and not care a thing about you." Although hurtful, women need to accept this truth. Another element to consider is that women may fall in love several times throughout their life. Men, unlike women, will love very few women throughout their lives. Other than his mother, he will only give his heart to one or maybe two other women. This truth is important to realize because a man will go to the earth's end for these few special women. When you are one of these special women, you will receive his best efforts and experience what he is truly capable of giving. The question women must address is "why would you want to give a man a child if you are not one of these special women in his life?" Men treat these "special women" with a much higher regard than they treat other women. It would be such a shame to give a man a child who does not consider you one of these special women. Black women are committing to this unthinkable arrangement way too often. Being a man's baby momma is not a highly regarded position in his life. However, becoming a mother is one of the most important endeavors a woman will undertake. Why waste this experience on a man who is not your husband and one who does not think you are special to him? Also keep in mind, men tend to know if you are the woman for him and will decide rather quickly if they want to marry you or not. We have all heard the horror stories about the woman who wastes five to ten years of her life waiting for a man to "come around" or miraculously transform into the man she wants him to become, only to suffer heartbreak after the relationship ends. Insult is added to injury when her "soulmate" marries his next girlfriend after knowing her for less than a year. As Greg Behrendt advised in his book *He's Just Not That Into You*, don't "waste the pretty" hoping a man will eventually give you what you want. Don't waste those crucial years of your life when you look your best and your eggs are the healthiest on a man who's "not that into you." Furthermore, it is important to reiterate that having a man's child will not change the fact that he does not want a future with you. Don't settle for becoming a baby momma for a man who does not value you. Having children under these circumstances devalues you as a woman and should be considered unacceptable behavior to a queen. This should go without saying, but if a man doesn't love you, respect you or refuses to marry you, do not become his baby momma. You deserve better!

4. **If you Want A Child for Any of the Following Reasons, DON'T:** Keep in mind, the only reason to bring life into this world is because you have a lot to offer a child! The decision to have children should be based on what you can give, not what you can get. It should be the most selfless decision you will ever make in your life. Great parents will attest to the fact that raising children involves—parents giving and children taking—for a really long time! If you have invested enough (love, time, money, sleepless nights, grey hair, etc.) in your child, you

will finally get a return on your investment, 25 or more years later, when you witness your child functioning as a successful, productive and happy adult. This may sound insane but this is truly the purpose of parenting. It is a long journey of one-sided, hard work and sacrifice. If you decide to become a mother and are not prepared to give tirelessly you are making a mistake. Furthermore, do not have children for any of these common, selfish reasons:

    a. **To Fill A Void:** Make sure you do not have a child because you think it will fill a void or if you think the child will serve as a "means to an end." Do not have a child if you simply want "something" to love you. Some women may witness the loving bond between a mother and her child and desire the unconditional admiration and attachment a child harvests for their mother. Children hopelessly love their mother regardless of her character or actions. Even drug addicted mothers, as neglectful as they may be, are still adored and needed by their children. Women who feel they are in need of this kind of intense, unbreakable love may want to have a child to satisfy this need. In reality, the love these women are missing is self-love. Having a child to feel loved and needed is a terrible misuse of a child's love. Once again, having children must be a selfless act, in which you are ready to give without expectation. To become equipped with the mindset necessary to be a good mother, you must fully know and love yourself. It is not your child's responsibility to validate you or give you self-esteem. This is an unfair expectation to place on a child. Also, keep in mind many of your shortcomings, such as low self-esteem, are often unknowingly passed onto your child. As a result of observing your behavior, your child may absorb many of your mental and emotional issues whether you are aware of it or not. So, make sure you love yourself completely and have resolved or overcome any psychological and emotional issues or voids prior to becoming a mother. A child should never be used as a tool for deriving self-worth.

b. **To Get or Keep a Man:** Do not have a baby to get or keep a man. Having a child is a stressful and trying undertaking that can sabotage a weak or nonexistent "relationship." Because a lot of black men are products of single-parent homes, many of them may not grasp the full scope and responsibility of parenting a child. Many black men were raised without their fathers present in the home and find it, not only acceptable—but completely normal for the two of you to raise your child separately. He will have no objection to being in his child's life even if he has severed ties with you. So, do not fool yourself into believing you and your child are a package deal. A man can love his child and not care for you, so do not try to use a baby as leverage. If a man did not love you unconditionally prior to you having his baby, this situation may definitely make him hate your guts. Let's face it; a lot of men hate their baby mommas. Love and respect yourself enough not to play this role in a man's life. If having a family is what you are yearning for, always keep in mind that having a man's baby does not make the two of you a family. A union is achieved as a result of marriage, in which you assume your husband's last name. This is the first step toward having a family—it is not achieved by becoming his baby momma. The awful thought of birthing a child who carries a last name that is different from yours, should be reason enough to avoid making this mistake. Do not have a baby to get or keep a man because it won't work out in your favor.

c. **Because You Desire Change:** Some women may begin to feel bored with life or develop a desire for change as they approach their 30's. This feeling of being stuck or stagnant can be intensified for a woman if most of her friends have children. If you can identify with this need for something new, having a baby is absolutely not the answer. Children and especially teenagers need wise mothers who have earned intellect and wisdom through life experience. Becoming a mother is not how a woman "finds herself." The only way to counteract feeling stagnant is to challenge oneself to grow. This type of growth happens as result of following your dreams, setting difficult goals, achieving those goals, taking risks, making mistakes and overcoming them. Furthermore, it is life's challenges that force us to find our best selves. Having a baby will not guarantee you will become a better woman, it will only ensure you will become a busier woman. Life is about the lessons you learn throughout each of its phases. It is important to commit to each phase of life and learn from the teachable moments within each phase. For example, these phases may consist of learning how to master healthy relationships, learning how to be a good friend, learning how to obtain independence, enjoying being selfish, learning how to coexist or live with another person, etc. The growth a woman acquires from these experiences fosters the confidence and wisdom she will need to be a respectable and competent mother. Once again, feeling bored or unaccomplished will not be counteracted once you become a mother. Having a child you are responsible for may further highlight your shortcomings. Seeing a child's innocent face will make you want to provide the best life possible for your child. Creating a good life for your child requires a plan, adequate resources and a strong parental unit intact. Furthermore, having a child cannot precede "coming into your own" as a woman and building a life you can be proud to share with a child. Challenge yourself to become a person your future children will admire. If you find yourself craving change, this is an indication that you need to aim higher and establish more challenging goals for your life.

d. **Because The "Dick Is Good":** This should go without saying but if you want to have a man's baby because he is great at pleasing you in bed, you are terribly immature and motherhood should be the furthest thing from your mind. Having a good sexual relationship with a man is absolutely no indication that the two of you would make decent parents. If this is your circumstance, and you tend to get "caught up in the moment" during great sex, you need to be utilizing some form of birth control in addition to using protection. If you enjoy a man's sexual performance, a simple thank you is a sufficient way to express your gratitude. If you are feeling unusually generous, you can "take him to Red Lobster." However, giving him a child is extraneous and ridiculous.

If you are not yet a mother, it must be your duty to reduce the number of black children born to unwed mothers. We must reduce this number from 72 percent to less than 15 percent. This must be our common goal as black women! By doing so, we can enrich our lives, repair our family structure and improve the condition of the black community. Let's redefine "what is normal" for us. Let's set a new standard for how we structure our families. Let's love and respect ourselves enough to not bare children for men who do not value us enough to give us their last names. It is time to place the appropriate value on legacy and family. We must also love and respect our unborn children enough to give them good fathers in the home and provide them with a life experience that is happy and conducive to success. We are much better than the choices we have been making. It is up to our young queens to redirect the black community down a different path—a path characterized by honor, respect, discipline and pride—and one that refutes laziness, ignorance, mediocrity and recklessness.

This is truly sound advice for women who are not yet mothers. However, so many black women have already decided to tackle motherhood alone. Their journey and the choices they make when raising their children has a huge impact on the future of Black America. It is just as imperative, if not more imperative, that these women have the tools necessary to learn to love themselves adequately and raise their children in such a way that they will not perpetuate this cycle of broken families.

OOPS! I'M A BABY MOMMA...WHAT NOW?

If you are a single mother it is important to implement the following adjustments to ensure your child can avoid as much psychological damage as possible. (1) Work on improving and maintaining your child's relationship with his or her father, (2) work on building your self-esteem, (3) restructure your life's goals in a way that will advance your child's future (4) begin viewing dating appropriately and (5) take steps to ensure your child will not repeat the cycle of broken homes.

Work on Your Child's Relationship with Their Father: Do not undervalue the importance of the relationship between your child and his or her father. So long as he is not a physical threat or toxic to your child's development, you must make it an immediate priority to allow him to be an integral part of your child's life. Put personal issues aside and be the bigger person. Parenting entails selflessness. Regardless of whether your baby daddy understands this concept, it is now your obligation to initiate and maintain a civil and amicable relationship with him. Make it easy for your child's father to spend time with his son or daughter. If you are difficult to deal with or if you make your child's father "jump through hoops," he will be less inclined to see his child. Ultimately, children suffer the most when you deny them a relationship with their father. Also, don't expect your child's father to be an expert at organizing play dates and outings with his child. The fact that he got you pregnant out of wedlock is a sure sign he lacks the inclination to plan and strategize. Now is the time for you to step up and formulate a visiting schedule. This will take all the brainwork out of creating a co-parenting schedule to help your baby daddy commit to the plan. It may feel as though you are taking on most of the responsibility but women are usually more competent when organizing the child's schedule. Being upset about having to do more than him is counterproductive. What matters most is your child's wellbeing. Just suck it up and understand that this is one of many consequences of having a child before marrying a qualified man who loves you. It is imperative to remain mature and focused on doing what's best for your child. Having to interact with your baby daddy may be easier said than done, especially if he is not being nice, if he's dating other women or if he's paying little to no child support. Despite his behavior, he is entitled to quality time with his child. Living a life in which you are forced to get along with a man who may be intolerable may feel like punishment—because it is. Having a child by anyone other than your husband is abnormal and risky. This is why co-parenting with your baby daddy may often feel like torture. A woman's husband has willingly agreed to act as her partner but the role of a baby daddy offers no guarantees. You must exercise patience and try to make the best out of this trying circumstance. This is the price you must pay to create a well-adjusted and happy child, outside of a marriage. Sometimes, even if you've taken on more responsibility, created a co-parenting schedule and have agreed to behave amicably, some men still fail to be active in their children's lives. In this scenario, as a last ditch effort, you must reach out to his family, particularly his mother, to encourage her to convince him to fulfill his responsibilities. Even if you are not on speaking terms with your baby daddy, you must appoint a third party, such as a grandparent, to pass the child to him. You must do everything in your power to ensure your child has a relationship with their father. Although it may seem easier to exclude your baby daddy from your child's life to avoid drama, never allow your pride or settling for "whatever's easier," interrupt your child's development. Children need their fathers.

Improve Your Self-Esteem: This is an important process, not only for your child's development but it will also help you come to terms with your mistakes. You must accept that at some point in your life you were short-sighted enough to lie down and make a permanent, life altering decision under temporary feelings. It is important to recognize how your immaturity led to poor decision-making, so you may learn and grow from your mistakes. This is the time to confront your "old self" and commit to no longer being the type of person that would make such choices. Once you understand why you made this choice, you can heal yourself and become less inclined to repeat this behavior. It is time to grow up and address your self-esteem issues. Therapy can help you resolve any issues that may have caused your low self-esteem. If you suffered from abandonment issues caused by an absent father, it is helpful to discuss your feelings with a therapist. Therapy can help you come to terms with how you were affected or scarred by your father's absence. It will help you understand how your father's poor example affected your decision to choose an unfit man to parent your child. It will also help you realize that your father's absence was not your fault. If you need to confront your father to find closure, do so. By resolving your feelings of disappointment, you will be better equipped to help your child avoid developing low self-esteem and will prevent them from repeating your mistakes.

Restructure Your Goals: You must restructure your life's goals around your child. If you need to go back to school to get a better job and make more money, focus on that. If your child has not yet reached school entry age, research the most desirable school districts and devise a plan that will make living in that community a possibility. Work with your child's father to start a college savings plan for your child's future. Statistics reveal that college-educated people are less likely to become teen parents or have children prior to marriage. According to the Population Association of America, 74 percent of women and 70 percent of men between the ages of 26 to 31 who do not have a college degree will have at least one child out of wedlock. The more education an individual receives, the less likely they are to have a baby out of wedlock. So, emphasize the importance of education to your child to ensure they will lead a life with unrestricted opportunities. Limit your time on social media and stop concerning yourself with what your peers are doing. Align yourself with positive people who support your goals and help you remain on track. This crucial phase of rebuilding your life will require your complete focus. It is unhealthy for your psyche to compare this part of your journey to other people's lives. Stop wasting energy worrying about your "snap back" and trying to reach "MILF" status. Whether men find you sexually desirable is irrelevant. Rid yourself of distractions and cut back on unnecessary social escapades and dating. These activities are extraneous to you now. Your child deserves your full attention, and that is the least you can do for him or her. These sacrifices will be the most rewarding changes you will ever make in your life once you see the positive effects on your child.

Change Your Views on Dating: Later on, when your life is together and your child is mature enough, you can extend time to personal pleasures. As with all good parents, everything you partake in from now on should have your child's best interest in mind. This should also extend to your dating decisions. As a single mother, you must no longer find the men you used to date enticing or even compatible with your new lifestyle. Make sure your head is on straight

KEEPING YOUR CROWN

and prevent another unplanned pregnancy at all costs! As a smarter woman, you must become marriage oriented to avoid accumulating multiple children by multiple fathers. Be realistic about what type of man is a good man for your circumstances. When you are ready to date, you should only consider grown men with the same attributes you possess. It is critical that you only entertain mature men, who are seeking a wife and marriage. Also, you may find that a man with a child or children is more compatible with your lifestyle and will better suit your needs—just make sure he is adequately providing for the child or children he already has. When a woman is dating the right man for her, the compatibility will be evident and a sense of easiness will be present in the relationship. Contrary to your past experiences, you will feel appreciated. Small things that were undervalued in the past, such as your domestic prowess, will finally be appreciated. Your cooking and cleaning abilities will finally come in handy with this man who appreciates your efforts because he is actually looking for a wife. You will no longer find yourself "playing wifey" and pulling out all of your "domestic tricks" for a man who eats your food and leaves to the next woman's house like your baby daddy used to do. Once you've gotten your life together, made your child your complete priority, made amends with your child's father, and are finally viewing dating appropriately, you are on the path to ensuring you have not damaged your child in such a way that he or she is likely to repeat your mistakes.

Break the Cycle: Make it your life's purpose to raise your children to become good people who are disciplined, ambitious and hardworking despite their circumstances. Raise your children to value education from an early age to ensure they make choices that advance both their lives and our community. Advancing the black community must be a common goal within your household. Teach your children to love being black and to love their black brothers and sisters. Ensure they understand how raising children within a broken home adversely affects the black community to prevent them from perpetuating this cycle once they reach adulthood. Make it a point to teach your children about love. Although they may not have witnessed a functioning marriage between you and their father, they need to understand the importance of compromise, sacrifice and respect between two people. As your children mature, emphasize the value of loving, respectful relationships and make sure they are marriage oriented. Emphasize the importance of taking each generation "up a notch." Make sure your children understand they must be married before they start their families and they must provide their children with a better life experience than they had.

Continue to be honest with yourself concerning the potential hazards you and your child will face and develop strategies to overcome these threats successfully. Understand that your child will need positive role models, mentors and extra motivation to compensate for the resources or guidance he or she may lack. Keep in mind, as the only parent in the home, your influence on your children is monumental. Make a valiant effort to work on your self-esteem and building your self-worth. Be conscious of how you treat yourself so you can show your children how to love themselves. Always remember, your children's future depends on your ability to equip them with the tools they need to succeed. Do everything in your power to prevent your sons and daughters from becoming statistics and perpetuators of the cancerous cycle of broken-homes that are taking over our communities. It is your responsibility to make sure you raise your children to become assets and not liabilities to society.

When a behavior occurs repeatedly—good or bad—over time, people often become desensitized and may accept that behavior as "normal." However, it is not normal or productive for a woman to raise children alone. The fact that black women have gradually accepted the idea of single motherhood clearly makes a statement about the condition of our self-esteem. To eradicate the single motherhood epidemic we must also repair our self-esteem.

"Everything that happens to you is a reflection of what you believe about yourself. We cannot outperform our level of self-esteem. We cannot draw to ourselves more than we think we are worth." –Iyanla Vanzant

The way many black women are having children implies we do not think we are deserving of love, marriage and a proper pregnancy and this realization is heartbreaking. If one could visualize a scenario of the ideal pregnancy—which every woman deserves and should want for herself—it would look something like this: You and your husband are elated to learn the news of your new baby. You have a comfortable lifestyle, with adequate resources and a beautiful nursery is awaiting your baby's arrival. As your tummy grows and you gain the weight necessary to carry a healthy baby, your husband thinks you are beautiful and is nervously overprotective of you during this process. When you deliver your baby, your husband is present during the delivery to hold your hand, while anticipating the extension to your growing family. Your husband thinks you are a hero and a superwoman for giving him a child!

Any woman who doesn't demand this level of support when bringing children into this world doesn't think highly of herself. Additionally, any woman who has never even contemplated what type of experience she demands during her pregnancy and is obliviously willing to "take life as it comes," should be on birth control. As black women, and as queens, we deserve nothing short of a loving, respectful, supportive partnership with a comfortable lifestyle before we bare children. To accept anything less is disrespectful to yourself, your legacy and will adversely impact the black community. Black women must redefine "what is normal" in terms of the way in which we experience motherhood. The lack of regard many black women delegate to motherhood is simply no longer acceptable. The way in which we bring life into this world is a direct reflection of how we value our lives, our bodies and our legacies. As queens, in order to "Keep Your Crown," we must regard ourselves and motherhood with the amount of value and respect it deserves.

> *"When you undervalue what you do, the world will undervalue who you are."* –Oprah Winfrey

SECTION FOUR: CHALLENGE TO OUR QUEENS

- **With 72% of black children being born to unwed mothers, young black queens must pledge to structure their families properly, giving their legacies the respect they deserve! As queens, we must redefine "what is normal" and commit to ONLY giving children to our husbands!!! We must admit, 72% is an astounding, embarrassing and an unacceptable percentage and we must**

acknowledge our responsibility to reduce this number!!!
- Construct a mental image of how you want to be perceived in society and make life choices that are in alignment with that image.
- The decision to become a mother should be the most responsible and selfless choice a woman will ever make so DO NOT have a baby to: fill a void in your life, to keep a man, because you feel bored or stagnant or because the "D" was good.
- If you are a single mother, never underestimate the importance of your child's relationship with his or her father. Do everything in your power to ensure this relationship is intact.
- For single mothers raising girls, understand that our young queens are more likely to perpetuate the cycle of broken homes if they are raised without their fathers. Exert effort into ensuring your daughter's relationship with her father or father figure is solid to prevent her from repeating your mistake.

- For single mothers raising black boys, understand, there are systems in place which profit from the mass incarnation of black men. Don't assist "the system" in allowing our young kings to fall victim to this process by denying their need for fathers and positive role models.
- Single mothers—refrain from introducing your children to your boyfriends. The "revolving door" of men coming in and out of your child's life will intensify their abandonment issues.
- Single mothers—your children are not your "friends." Our black children need discipline and positive examples to grow into respectable, productive adults. Don't limit their potential by denying them the structure they need to be successful.
- Single mothers—love yourself and constantly work on building your self-esteem. You show your children how to treat themselves, so carry yourself with the upmost respect and dignity.

SECTION FIVE:
MANAGING OUR SELF-IMAGE

Be Educated · Be Selfish · Be Healthy · Be Cultured

5

SECTION FIVE:

MANAGING OUR SELF-IMAGE

"Only make decisions that support your self-image, self-esteem and self-worth."

–Oprah Winfrey

Black women are extremely influential in our communities. We have direct influence over what type of adults our children will become as a result of how we raise them and what values we instill in them. We show men how to treat us according to how we treat ourselves. When we treat ourselves well, we set high standards that men are willing to match because they are motivated by a good woman's approval. Good women greatly influence a man's standards for how he treats women and how hard he is willing to work for his family. Considering the revered position black women hold in the lives of their men and children, this responsibility must be taken seriously. It is important for black women to understand that we are vital assets to our community and when at our best, the value we add is indispensable. With this in mind, it is our responsibility to ensure we are thriving in every aspect of our lives. Specifically, it is important for black women to focus on: (1) being educated (2) being selfish (3) being healthy and (4) being cultured.

BE EDUCATED

The first and most important way to ensure our success is by equipping ourselves with an education. As previously mentioned, black women deserve acclaim for their notable academic accomplishments. We must not only maintain this level of success, but we must also continue encouraging black women to be highly educated and accomplished. Regardless of whether your aspirations in life are to be a judge or a housewife, the decision to educate yourself should be mandatory. This does not necessarily imply that receiving further education after high school is mandatory—although it's highly encouraged. This simply means, if additional schooling is not a requirement for your particular career or life path; continue educating yourself on your own. Even if you are not in school, you should read daily. You should find subjects that interest you, study them and learn new ideas. As a queen, it is your personal responsibility to be articulate, well read and well versed. Additionally, even if you are not a business woman, a queen should have a firm handshake and make proper eye contact. These gestures demand respect and imply that a woman is confident and self-assured.

    Black women must respect and acknowledge the sacrifices our ancestors made to ensure our right to receive an education. Black people have endured a violent, insufferable and disadvantaged history in this country. In our not-so-distant past, black people were killed for attempting to read or educate themselves. We owe it to our ancestors to take full advantage of the opportunities for which they died. It is ignorant and disrespectful to your legacy to deny yourself an education now that we are afforded the opportunity. For those same reasons, it is also imperative that we exercise our right to vote in every single election. Do not take our ancestors' sacrifices for granted. Do not become lazy and complacent. Do not devalue the opportunities they afforded us, which cost many of them their lives. In life, an education is the only equalizer that can assist you in transcending your socioeconomic position and should never be undervalued.

Additionally, we live in a generation that often places little emphasis on intellect—but to the contrary—it is important to value an education now more than ever. Making yourself valuable is essential to the success of your family, your community and this country. You add value when you educate yourself. You add value when you acquire a useful skill and become of service to society by becoming a doctor, a professor, a soldier, a senator, a dermatologist, a CPA, a pilot, etc. The world does not benefit from having a plethora of uneducated people who have no desire to be of service to others. Do not be fooled by the media, social media or similar outlets that constantly promote talentless, shallow "instant celebrities" who are famous for simply "being famous." These institutions profit from encouraging and perpetuating ignorance, narcissism and salacious behavior. Although Americans have become terribly desensitized to worshiping toxic ideals and unworthy people, we have to reexamine our values and raise our standards for what behaviors and role models we deem respectable.

BE SELFISH

This may sound like unconventional or irresponsible advice but it is important for women to reevaluate the way they perceive "being selfish." Women tend to have a hard time telling people "no." As nurturers, we feel obligated to be there for people. We often place the needs of others before our own. However, we have to put our wants and needs first if we want true happiness and success. The fact of the matter is our loved ones, our co-workers and our communities will benefit more when we bring our best selves forward. This is accomplished when you take time to nurture yourself and make yourself your main priority. Take your passions and goals seriously and devote more time to building personal success. Make sure that finding and fulfilling your purpose is a mandatory responsibility. Do what you need to be happy and neglect the notion that being selfish is a bad thing. Particularly, women are encouraged to consider being selfish in these following areas: (1) when dating (2) with your vagina and (3) with your finances.

Be Selfish When Dating: Being selfish is especially important in our dating lives and when dealing with men. Men unapologetically have a self-centered and self-preserving approach towards life. They make decisions based on what is best for them and what makes them happy. They rarely allow people to guilt them into doing things they do not want to do. This may be attributable to testosterone, pride or a lack of emotions but when dating, men seem to be experts at disallowing someone to hurt or disrespect them without consequence. They are incredibly protective of their feelings and typically will not allow someone the opportunity to hurt them continuously. It seems reasonable to assume that because women are more emotionally fragile, we would exercise the same, if not more caution when guarding our hearts. However, when dating, women typically use their emotions to their own detriment. We tend to think with our hearts and avoid logic when making decisions. If we want to ensure we are achieving success in every aspect of life, we have to start loving ourselves more. We have to start loving ourselves as much as men love themselves. We have to be just as selfish and over-protective of our hearts and feelings. This is no implication that we should be guarded or closed off when dating but we should not allow our emotions to cloud our judgement. When dating we have to set boundaries for what we will and will not put up with and disallow second chances if someone crosses that boundary. We have to feel comfortable being demanding about what we feel we deserve, just as men do.

Although men are incredibly self-serving, their selfishness is counter-balanced by how much they love and adore selfish women. Women may find it difficult to believe that men love selfish women, but they really, really do! Men are simplistic when determining how they should treat a woman, to what degree they respect her, and how to love her. They will simply treat you exactly how you treat yourself. Men will not question if how you feel about yourself is true or false. They will simply follow your lead. Men find women who take immaculate care of themselves completely irresistible. If you carry yourself like a lady, men will presume you are a lady. If you treat yourself with respect, men will respect you. If you believe your wants and needs are important, men will agree with you. So, make sure you treat yourself well, considering you show others how to treat you.

Be Selfish With Your Vagina: While on the topic of being selfish, it is important that women understand the power they possess by having vaginas. This is also known as "the power of the P." When a woman properly understands the value her vagina adds to her life, she can better use it to enhance her life. Essentially, the vagina has two phases. The first phase consists of using it for sexual pleasure and to control men. The second phase involves using your vagina as a miraculous vessel to produce life. The vagina's role throughout both phases is important and instrumental in a woman's life. It is important to respect both phases and is

KEEPING YOUR CROWN

especially important to be selfish during both phases of the vagina. "Men are sexual by nature and women are emotional by nature" according to Kara King, author of *The Power of the Pussy*. The fact that men need sexual pleasure from women makes the vagina, to some degree, a commodity. Once a woman understands her body's worth, she has control and leverage over men that can truly enhance her life. Men enjoy chasing and pursing women. Withholding sex during the chase is when women have the most leverage. According to Kara King, "In all honesty, he's most likely going to get sex somewhere else if he's not getting it from you. This is still GOOD! While he's using some other woman for sex, he's thinking about you and what it will take to get you to be his girl. She'll be the quick piece of ass and you'll be the woman that gives him butterflies in his stomach. He'll use her for sex, while you're receiving flowers and going out on nice dates. She'll be the one hurt in the end, while you'll be "the one" who makes him fall in love." It serves a woman best to share her body with a man who loves her. This important detail can prevent a woman from being used or hurt.

KEEPING YOUR CROWN

During the first phase of the vagina, women are encouraged to experience and enjoy making love. It is natural and healthy for a woman to enjoy intimacy within a loving and respectful relationship. Keep in mind, change is inevitable. So, for women who may want children in the future, enjoy this sexy time in life! Enjoy the luxury of being able to sleep in and make love all day without the pitter patter of your little rug rats swarming around and ruining the mood. This is also a special time to gain sexual experience and learn your body. Being great at sex will definitely come in handy! It is during this phase, women mature sexually and understand that sex can be casual so long as your partner is respectful and enhances your life in some way. To a woman's advantage, there are generous men out there who enjoy spoiling confident women who understand their vagina's worth. During this phase it is completely acceptable to allow a man to experience the pleasure of your vagina in exchange for mutual adoration and life's comforts. If a nice, successful gentleman is in favor of enhancing your life substantially, allow him to— you deserve it! Women are encouraged to enjoy the perks of the phase one vagina in a respectful and mature manner.

KEEPING YOUR CROWN

In most cases, the vagina is at its best prior to having children. Let's face it child birth can take its toll on the vagina. After a vaginal birth, the vagina is looser and due to hormonal changes, your libido will be lower and sometimes nonexistent. So during the first phase of the vagina, it is important for a woman to exclusively and selfishly, only share her "power" with men who respect her, treat her well, and enhance the comforts of her life. It is important for a woman to know her worth and refrain from having sexual relationships with men who treat her like shit. Respecting yourself and your vagina will allow a woman to experience the best a man has to offer. Eventually, a very special man who adores you and loves you unconditionally will sweep you off of your feet. If you choose to marry him, you may likely transition to the second phase of the vagina.

While phase one of the vagina entails having fun, learning your body, deriving pleasure, controlling men and enjoying adoration, gifts and other perks, phase two serves a much higher purpose. Phase two embodies the ultimate sacrifice of a woman's body in exchange for an extraordinary blessing. In this phase of the vagina, a woman has found her life partner who loves her entirely and unconditionally. At this point it will be rewarding to bless your lucky husband with children. In phase two your vagina will serve as a vessel to bring new life into this world to grow your family and nothing is more beautiful than this!

One would think a woman would be selfish during both phases and especially during phase two. Unfortunately, this is not always the case. Some women monumentally screw up phase two by sacrificing their vaginas for men who are not their husbands. It is unacceptable to give a man a child if he doesn't love or care about you. It is also important to remember, having sex with a man or having his baby is not how a woman gains leverage. Women gain leverage by withholding sex until they get what they want. If a woman shares her vagina too soon, a man may have no incentive to comply with her needs. Realistically, a man gains complete leverage when a woman consents to becoming his baby momma. When a woman becomes a baby momma and is still single, she places herself at a disadvantage in the event she is still in search of a husband but with a phase two vagina and another man's child. It is not as easy to use the phase two vagina to take advantage of the benefits available to the phase one vagina. You may encounter opposition from men if you try to use sex as leverage to control men after you've already used your vagina to have another man's child.

It is important that a woman's mind and body are in alignment. Your mind state and direction in life should coincide or comply with the phases of the vagina. The phase one vagina best serves a single or unwed woman. The phase two vagina is conducive to better serving a married woman who is in a committed marriage and is no longer "playing the field." If your mentality is that of a single woman and dating and having an enjoyable sex life is still your priority, it is a huge mistake to allow your vagina to enter into phase two, if your mindset is still in phase one. It is counterproductive to alter your lifestyle and body, knowing you are still single, unwed and "playing the field." A single mentality and a phase two vagina are not harmonious.

KEEPING YOUR CROWN

Some women take this mistake a step further by not only failing to preserve their vagina for their husband but by also giving a man a child who is not financially fit to be a father. The thought of having children by anyone other than your husband is bad enough, but it is a catastrophic mistake to have a baby by a man who is broke. Because your vagina is valuable, it does not make sense to sleep with a man who would ultimately abandon you, thus making you solely, financially responsible for your child. It is a disturbing reality that some women even rely on welfare or some form of government assistance to survive. A woman should never have a child with a man who is not taking care of her. It should be a cardinal sin to have sex with "bums," let alone have a baby with one. When committing this unthinkable mistake you are essentially "bankrupting" your vagina. This is the ultimate misuse of the vagina so avoid it at all costs! Making a conscious decision to become a man's baby momma—especially if he is mean to you or broke—defies the laws of "the power of the P." With this in mind, maintain your selfishness and protect your precious vagina as if it were gold—because it is! As a queen, you must treat your vagina like royalty!

Be Selfish With Your Finances: Obtaining financial independence is another important component of being selfish. Financial independence allows women to experience unrestricted freedom and plays a crucial role in a woman's evolution. Women who are financially dependent do not mature and develop at the same level as financially independent women. A woman who possesses financial literacy and can take care of herself is more mature and confident. Being financially dependent on a man can be an unstable existence for a woman. When a man is in a position of power and has the ability to abuse his power, it is likely he will. Within relationships, the person with financial dominance or "the power of the purse" has more control. So if a woman does not feel secure in giving a man too much control, she should make it a priority to have her own money.

It is important for women to understand this concept as early as possible. Women should practice financial independence as soon as they move out of their parents' home. It is important to experience living alone and paying your own bills prior to living with your husband. Living with roommates (perhaps during or after college) is also helpful for gaining self-awareness. Having a roommate(s) will provide insight as to what type of house mate you are and if you are even tolerable as a mate. In her younger years, it is also advantageous for a woman to refrain from living with boyfriends and "playing house." This is not a stable living arrangement for a young woman. If the relationship gets rocky, as young relationships tend to, it is crucial that a young woman have her own place to retreat to and remove herself from problematic situations.

One of the main reasons women should acquire financial stability is to avoid disrespect or abuse. One of the worst situations a woman can place herself in, is relying on a man for a place to live (or some other source of stability) and subjecting herself to disrespect she wouldn't tolerate otherwise. If a man is mean to you, he deserves to be kicked to the curb. A woman must be in a position to leave a man if he behaves poorly. Leaving an immature man is the only way to enforce your boundaries while teaching him what behaviors are unacceptable. Do not allow yourself to be subjected to behavior you don't deserve because you cannot stand on your own two feet. Make sure you have enough resources to leave a man if he is not making your life comfortable and enjoyable.

It is important for a woman to know herself and what degree of financial leverage she needs in a relationship. If you are a woman who enjoys working, is good at making money and needs a certain level of independence to feel comfortable and secure, do not sacrifice your career or financial independence for a man or marriage. A man who truly loves you will be in awe of your success and will support your endeavors. Furthermore, if you have a low threshold for aggressive behavior or chauvinistic tendencies from men, protect yourself by ensuring that you are financially self-sufficient. This assurance allows you to avoid dealing with a man's BS because you won't need him to survive.

Successful women must keep in mind they should not speak of their financial situation to anyone other than their financial planner. This is especially important for wealthy women. Don't flaunt or brag about your financial success. This behavior is tasteless and crude. The point of financial freedom is to protect yourself and your happiness.

It is not intended as a means to belittle others or emasculate men. It is terribly unattractive to brag to men about your assets or financial standing. Remember, one beautiful quality good men possess is their lack of concern with how little or how much money you have. Grown men believe in building their own wealth and providing for their loved ones. So by flaunting her wealth, a woman will surely offend good men. On the other hand, being boastful about your finances will attract a different caliber of men—con artists and scammers. These low-life men—who may likely have daddy issues—would absolutely love to be taken care of by a woman. Only ill-intentioned men would concern themselves with a woman's bank account. For this reason women are encouraged to keep their finances to themselves.

If you are a woman who is more traditional in terms of gender roles and prefers for her man to act as the sole provider, it is still necessary to familiarize yourself with the family finances. Even if you do not work, never leave yourself in the dark concerning the finances. Make it a point to always know what's going on with your money. As an adult, you need to have access to your accounts and you need to know how to pay bills. Choosing to be ignorant of your financial standing is childish and dangerous. If you are comfortable allowing your mate to act as the sole provider, make sure you choose a man who is kind and will never use his financial control to influence your behavior or choices. Make sure he is not the type of man who will "wave" the lifestyle he provides for you over your head. Real men will not engage in this type of unacceptable behavior because taking care of his woman is what a man is expected to do.

Much of this advice is directed toward younger women considering most black women are no strangers to being financially independent. Keeping in mind the considerably high rate of single mothers, most black women are left with no other option than supporting her family alone. This is an unfortunate introduction to financial management where a woman has no choice but to be the sole provider for her family. In this instance, financial independence was forced as a means of survival. This circumstance does not provide the euphoric feeling of freedom that financial independence provides for single women. Once again, to truly enjoy the benefits of financial independence, women should set financial goals prior to being married and most certainly, prior to having children.

KEEPING YOUR CROWN

There is no better feeling than the satisfaction generated by making your own money. This independence greatly improves a woman's level of self-esteem and self-confidence. Furthermore, when women understand what it feels like to earn their own money, they'll be more gracious when a man adequately provides for her or compliments her lifestyle. Spoiled girls tend to act like money "grows on trees" and may lack appreciation for the lengths men go to, to provide us with nice things because they've never worked for anything. It should be every woman's goal to avoid being financially naïve because it is girlish, immature and terribly unattractive. Regardless of what stance you may take on this issue, be aware of the advantages and freedoms that being financially selfish can provide!

Although it is second nature for women to place others before ourselves, we must adopt the concept of "being selfish" into our lives! It is important for women to understand the value of being selfish when dating, when using our vaginas and when controlling our finances. The only instance in which sacrificing your happiness and being selfless is acceptable and expected is when it benefits your children. Good mothers must forfeit their wants and happiness for their children's best interests. This is a harsh reality because you may experience some suffering while doing what is best for your child but children deserve your selflessness because they do not ask to be here. This may be a tough concept to accept because being selfish is so enjoyable. So, it is important to reinforce waiting to have children until you are completely ready to sacrifice your selfishness. Prior to motherhood, enjoy the luxury of being selfish as long as you possibly can!

BE HEALTHY

When striving to create a life that is well-rounded and well balanced, attention to your health is vitally important. When even one aspect of your health is impaired, it can impact all other areas of your life. In order to focus on your goals and your purpose, you cannot be stifled by serious health issues that are preventable. As black women, we have a tendency to overlook our health because we applaud being thick and curvy. While it is commendable that we embrace our bodies and no longer fall victim to societal standards of beauty, we must place greater emphasis on being healthy. There are four components that require more attention while on our path to achieving better health: (1) "our numbers" (2) our diet (3) our exercise regime and (4) our mental health.

"Our Numbers": In this instance "our numbers" refers to waist size, BMI (body mass index) and blood pressure. It is important to know your waist size because it is a direct reflection of your overall health. The ideal waist size for women is 32 ½ inches or smaller. If your waist size is 35 inches or larger, your chances for acquiring chronic illnesses like heart disease and diabetes can increase. Your BMI is a good indication of whether you are in a healthy weight range (you can go online to find the formula to arrive at your BMI). Whether BMI is accurate for black people is a question often asked. Some studies show that blacks tend to have less visceral fat (the fat located around the organs) and more muscle mass, so it is possible that our BMI range might be slightly different. So, if you discredit using BMI when critiquing your health, your waist size and blood pressure are still accurate indicators. Knowing your blood pressure is important because it reveals your likelihood of suffering from harmful conditions like cardiovascular disease or stroke. Unfortunately, blacks are diagnosed with high blood pressure more often than other demographics. Whether this diagnosis is due to genetics, stress or being overweight, it is important to know your blood pressure. If your systolic pressure (the top number) is too high (over 140) consult with your doctor to find the appropriate measures to take to arrive at a healthy blood pressure.

Our Diet: Your diet is one component that has the biggest impact on your overall health. The expression "food is medicine" is monumentally true and is the best preventive measure to take for averting disease. The opposite is also true; "food" can be poison. Although it requires immense discipline and initially may not be much fun, it is imperative for black women to give dieting the effort it deserves. While transitioning to a healthier lifestyle, there are foods that must be eliminated altogether and foods that should only be consumed on occasion. The foods that need to be eliminated are fast food, processed foods and soda (Keep in mind, some fast food restaurants have improved the quality of their ingredients but many are still using processed meats and other mystery ingredients. So, be sure to do your due diligence and research when determining which restaurants to avoid and which restaurants serve healthier options). Processed foods are items that are usually packaged in boxes, cans or bags. To become edible, these foods are processed extensively and are not found as is, in nature. Fast food, processed foods and soda have little or no nutritional value and are dangerous to your health. Fast food and processed foods alike contain preservatives or chemicals that slow down the food's decomposition to make them last longer on grocery shelves or in fast food restaurants. These preservatives are harmful and foreign to your body. The human body is not designed to break down these chemicals as it would "real food." When these substances accumulate in your body, they can lead to sickness and cancer. Sodas too, must be eliminated. Because of the large amounts of sugar and artificial sweeteners added for flavor, along with other artificial ingredients, soda is more harmful than people may be aware. The excessive consumption of sugar is extremely dangerous and is also highly addictive. Sodas are also one of the major contributors to obesity in America. For these reasons, most fast food, processed food and soda should be eliminated from your diet. A few helpful hints for making grocery shopping more productive and free of processed items are to read the ingredients. If there are over ten ingredients on the label or if you can't pronounce the ingredient items, they are probably loaded with preservatives and other chemicals that are harmful to your body. Also, most packaged snacks are loaded with "fake stuff." Try sticking to options that are fresh and expire rather quickly. Foods that "go bad" quickly are essentially "real food," free of preservatives and other cancer causing chemicals. So make it a habit to load up on fruits, vegetables, nuts and lean protein instead of packaged, processed garbage, posing as real food.

Foods that can be enjoyed on occasion or on "cheat days" are fried food, read meat (pork and beef), sweets/deserts and white/refined carbohydrates (rice, bread, pasta and potatoes). Although these foods taste good, when consumed in excess, they can cause unfavorable effects on your health. Fried foods are high in saturated fats and promote bad cholesterol. When eating them in excess, you may experience severe weight gain, acne, high blood pressure and may become at risk for diabetes. When consumed in excess, red meats, like steaks and beef burgers, can take a toll on your body. They harden blood vessels putting you at risk for atherosclerosis, they increase your risk for diabetes and can cause an excess of iron that can affect the brain, leading to Alzheimer's. Red meat is also difficult to digest which can lead to colorectal cancer and is often full of harmful hormones that can cause other cancers. Pork is high in fat, higher than beef and chicken. As with all fatty foods, eating an excess of pork can cause obesity, high cholesterol, high blood pressure, heart problems and cancer. Sweets and deserts are loaded with sugar and as already mentioned can destroy the body. Not only can sugar lead to tooth decay but heavy consumption can also cause obesity and blood sugar spikes, triggering health problems like diabetes. Similarly, white/refined carbohydrates like pasta and bread contain little natural nutrients because they undergo processing which removes many of their essential vitamins and minerals. They also break down into sugar and can cause severe weight gain. On that note, although these foods are enjoyable, moderation is the key. It may not be necessary to deprive oneself of these foods but understand that discipline and restraint is a must. Limiting your intake of these items to one cheat day a week can improve your overall health and can add years to your life. The immediate satisfaction gained when eating these tasty foods can be short lived when the side effects come into play.

Substitution is an amazing tool to implement to "trick" oneself into making healthier nutritional choices without feeling deprived. Substitution means finding a healthier, yet equally satisfying food selection to benefit your overall health. There are plenty of options available to make this process easy. By simply replacing beef burgers for chicken, turkey or veggie patties can make a substantial difference. These alternatives are a leaner source of protein and contain 50% less fat than beef burgers. Try replacing sodas with flavored sparking water to reduce your sugar intake and to eliminate hundreds of empty calories from your daily diet. Baked sweet potato fries are a tasty substitute for French fries. Sweet potatoes and are rich in vitamins, minerals, and iron and are effective at preventing certain cancers. Whole wheat and whole grain options are wonderful substitutes for white/refined carbohydrates, especially on days that aren't cheat days. They are loaded with vitamins and minerals and are high in fiber which makes them digest slowly, keeping us full much longer and helps control blood sugar levels. Common and delicious options include whole wheat or whole grain bread, brown rice, quinoa, and whole wheat pasta. In addition to those alternatives, try substituting vegetables for carbs like making spaghetti squash instead of regular spaghetti, using lettuce wraps for buns or tortillas and making cauliflower mash instead of mashed potatoes. When implementing these changes, your overall appearance and energy levels will drastically improve. Learning how to make healthy alternatives at home will encourage you to get back in the kitchen and take control of what you are putting into your body—not to mention it will keep money in your pockets. Let's face it, dieting sucks at first. So, the objective is to develop reasonable and healthy eating habits to avoid being on an actual diet. It is somewhat unrealistic to avoid the "cheat foods" altogether, but try to consume them as infrequently as possible to achieve optimum health.

Another factor to consider while grocery shopping is that, the FDA approves many food processing practices that are unhealthy and sometimes deadly. So although it may be pricier, try purchasing organic produce and "happy" meat. Organic produce is free of pesticides, synthetic fertilizers and genetically modified organisms (GMOs) and lessens your exposure to these potentially harmful substances. "Happy" meats are meats from animals bred in free range, grass-fed and organic environments. These animals are not raised in farming factories or slaughter houses that practice animal cruelty, torture or other poor practices. It is important to avoid eating inorganic meats to reduce consumption of hormones, steroids and high levels of antibiotics. One common mistake people make when attempting to eat healthy is unknowingly eating dangerous "farm-raised" fish. Although one may think fish is a healthy option, it is not always the case in America. Be sure to stay away from fish that is "farm-raised" or "farm-bred" and stick to fresh, wild caught fish. Fish that are commonly raised in fish farms are tilapia, salmon, catfish, sea bass and cod. According to DrAxe.com, fish raised in fish farms contain high concentrations of antibiotics and pesticides, cause as much inflammation in the body as bacon, have lower levels of healthy nutrients and contain ten times the amount of cancer causing pollutants than the wild caught breeds. So avoid this common "healthy" eating mistake. When searching for these items in stores look for packaging labels such as "Organic," "Wild Caught," "Certified Humane Raised & Handled" and "Freedom Food" to ensure you are making safer produce, meat and fish selections.

The key to maintaining good health is to improve the small choices we make every day. Here are a few small adjustments you can make daily to improve your overall health. Smoothies and juicing are a great way to get the appropriate daily servings of fruits and vegetables in a way that is quick, delicious and convenient. Considering time constraints, it is difficult for most of us to consume the recommended servings of fruits and vegetables. This is the most efficient way to ensure you are getting the nutrients you need. Even when we attempt to have a well-balanced diet, it is still difficult to get all the vitamins and nutrients we need so taking a daily multivitamin is important. Another easy way to achieve improved health is by drinking a tablespoon of apple cider vinegar every morning. There are countless benefits of this old, household remedy including curing an upset stomach, aiding in digestion, aiding in weight loss, soothing a sore throat, lowering blood sugar levels to help with diabetes, etc. Another simple, yet beneficial habit to adopt is drinking tea. Different teas provide different benefits, so enjoy experimenting with different blends and flavors to discover what suits your needs. Tea provides the following health benefits: it contains antioxidants, it helps with digestion and weight loss, it boosts the immune system and helps battle some cancers. Lastly, it is important to make sure you hydrate properly. Because your body needs adequate fluid to perform almost every bodily function, skimping on the recommended amount of water is not an option. In addition to getting the proper amount of water, also try drinking lemon water for detoxifying purposes and coconut water for additional hydration. These small changes to your daily routine can improve your overall health and require minimal effort to maintain.

Having a healthy diet serves women in more ways than one. Yes, having a healthy diet can elongate and enrich a woman's quality of life but it can also improve her physical appearance and bodily functions. Many of the key nutrients found in fruits and vegetables are the nutrients needed for healthy hair, skin and nails. Beauty starts on the inside and developing healthy eating habits will certainly enhance a woman's physical beauty. Another benefit of healthy eating women may overlook is how it can assist in keeping the vagina PH balanced. According to *How Your food Impacts Your Vagina* by Aleisha Fetters on WomensHealthMag.com, women should consider themselves eating for two, you and your vagina. Women should indulge in fruits, veggies, whole grains, plenty of water and Greek yogurt to maintain a healthy acidic PH and balance. This article also suggests that women with uncontrolled high blood sugar due to diabetes can become at risk for yeast infections and should cut back on sugar for the vagina's sake. So it is important for women to be aware that indulging in junk food can wreck your body and health as well as the wellbeing of your vagina. In other words, a woman can't scarf down soda, nuggets and fries and expect to have a balanced and fragrant vajayjay!

KEEPING YOUR CROWN

Our Exercise Regime: There is no need to sell the benefits of exercise. We all know exercise is completely necessary to maintain a good quality of life. So, making the choice to be inactive is simply unacceptable. Black women have a tendency to undervalue exercise and it typically ranks low on their list of priorities. Exercise constantly takes a back seat to our duties as mothers, our careers, our commitment to maintaining our hair styles and our insistence on "preserving our curves." But these excuses are not valid and should no longer be the reason we are not living our best lives. It is your responsibility as a queen to value your body as your temple and give yourself the care you deserve. People will make time for activities they consider important, so having a "busy schedule" is no excuse if getting healthy is your priority. An effective workout may only require 30 to 45 minutes of your day, three to five times a week. Specifically, women need up to 30 minutes of cardio such as cycling, speed walking or running coupled with toning exercises like lifting weights. It is also important for women to increase the intensity of weight training gradually as we get older. If you are lost and confused in the gym, hiring a personal trainer or participation in group classes can give you direction. This is such a small commitment considering the value it adds to your life, health and confidence.

Our Mental health: The mind and the body have an intense interconnectedness. Having a healthy mindset and a positive outlook is important because it impacts both your day-to-day interactions as well as your physical health. If you are stressed, anxious or depressed it is difficult to have meaningful connections with others which may stifle your productivity. If you experience a hard time muting negative thoughts and fears swarming in your head, it is hard to listen to the voice in your heart that is directing you toward success in finding your purpose. If you do not give the proper care and attention to your mental state, the effects may eventually impact your physical health in a variety of ways, such as migraines, ulcers, high blood pressure, a weakened immune system, weight gain or loss, and insomnia. There are several ways to protect your mental health but one of the best ways is by managing your stress. But first, let's begin by dividing stress into two categories: controllable stressors and uncontrollable stressors.

Controllable stressors include anything that causes stress that you have the power to alleviate altogether or stress you can alleviate by properly managing your emotions. Examples of controllable stressors are toxic people or relationships. If you find you have people in your life that are causing you strife and you have a say in whether they remain in your life, you have to remove those people and end those relationships. It is your obligation to yourself to only allow people in your space that are positive, kind, supportive, inspiring and enjoyable. If someone displays qualities to the contrary, end the relationship and terminate this controllable stressor. If there are people in your life who stress you or are emotionally disruptive and you cannot remove them from your life, like your baby daddy or a coworker for instance, you must learn to control your responses to them. This scenario still involves a controllable stressor because you can learn healthy ways to utilize self-control when interacting with unavoidable toxic people. It is your responsibility to preserve and protect your mental health and whether you allow others to steal your peace is solely up to you.

KEEPING YOUR CROWN

One great way to preserve your peace is to remain so focused on your goals and purpose that if anything or anyone one is not in alignment with them, consider it a distraction and do not give it your time or energy. Another way to protect your peace is by trying to understand the toxic individual's intentions before acknowledging his or her behavior. If the toxic person's intention was to upset you with his or her actions, having awareness of the fact that they enjoy seeing you upset should motivate you to do just the opposite. Don't lose your cool and become a pawn in their game. Brush off their childish antics and again, keep site of your goals and purpose. Sometimes the toxic person's actions are not intentional in upsetting or offending you. They may be ignorant or generally unhappy in their own life and are unknowingly projecting their hurt or anger towards you. In this situation, do not engage or take their behavior personally. Focus on yourself and work on mastering self-control and patience.

Unfortunately, in life there are also uncontrollable stressors. Uncontrollable stressors are unfortunate events that simply happen to us that we cannot control. Examples of these stressors include experiencing the death of a friend or family member, being laid off from a job or experiencing other financial hardship. Although we cannot control these unfortunate occurrences, we must find positive ways to overcome these events and rebuild ourselves. There are certain activities that can stimulate your mind and body in positive ways to help you survive these hardships without a mental breakdown. Cardio exercises like running can cause the central nervous system to release chemicals called endorphins that create positive feelings in the body and reduce your perception of pain. Meditation, deep breathing exercises and yoga are other activities that effectively quiet the mind, reduce anxiety, improve blood flow and increase serotonin levels. According to Healthline.com, serotonin is a chemical messenger that acts as a mood stabilizer. It can positively impact your mood, improve sleeping patterns and counteract depression. Reading a good book or watching a hilarious comedy is a good way to stimulate positive emotions and take your mind off of your problems. Therapy is always important for more intense stressors to find understanding and resolve. Also, surrounding yourself with positive, supportive and loving people can relieve the loneliness that may develop when struggling with life's battles. Life won't always be easy but our strength as black women has always proved true. Even at our weakest we are capable of great successes, but to achieve what we are truly capable of, we must strive for excellence in all areas of life, especially our health. We must give the proper attention to "our numbers," our diet, our exercise regime, and most certainly our mental well-being.

BE CULTURED

Black women are vital assets to the black community. The values we instill in our children and the standards we set for our men have the propensity to build the foundation for strong families and unbreakable communities. So, in addition to being educated, being selfish and being healthy, we must place the proper value on being cultured. There are few experiences that can elevate your perceptions and expand your mind the way travel does. As a valued leader, it is expected that a queen obtain knowledge and experiences that transcend her hometown. When a person experiences a life that is specific to one city, neighborhood, region or part of town, they tend to develop one way of thinking and one way of living. To become a well-rounded individual, it is necessary to experience places that are foreign to your way of thinking and your way of doing things. Traveling will allow you to experience contrast from your current life-experience and will allow you to better understand yourself and others. So, don't be basic. Have a passport to ensure you have the ability to travel at your leisure. The more we travel, the smaller the world becomes and we naturally become less small-minded. Allow yourself the opportunity to become more open-minded, initially through travel and then develop a general comfortability when exploring other new experiences! Try foods from other countries and cultures instead of always eating your usual cuisine to develop a more sophisticated palate. Hot wings and fried calamari cannot always be your "go-to" items on the menu every time you dine out! Study manners and etiquette, both American and foreign, so you may carry yourself with elegance despite your environment. Study and experience different wines instead of always ordering Moscato, considering it is a dessert wine and is typically consumed at that specific time! Expand your reading list and experiment with reading genres that differ from your usual reading style. Perhaps you can take more of an interest in art by finding pieces that speak to you and learn the history or story behind the piece.

"Find a beautiful piece of art. If you fall in love with Van Gogh or Matisse or John Oliver Killens, or if you fall in love with the music of Coltrane, the music of Aretha Franklin, or the music of Chopin—find some beautiful art and admire it..." –Maya Angelou

These are general examples but ultimately the motivation behind becoming more cultured is to enrich our lives. Being cultured allows us to explore new interests and experiences we may have overlooked had we remained immobile, small-minded and one-dimensional.

To serve as positive agents of change within our communities, black women must work on improving our self-image. We must continue regarding education with the upmost importance and further encourage our young queens to pursue postsecondary education. We must develop a new appreciation for being selfish. Specifically, we must be selfish when dealing with men, when valuing and understanding our vaginas and concerning our finances. We must understand that if our health is not a priority, it can adversely impact all other areas of our lives. We must pay attention to "our numbers," our diet, our exercise regime and our mental health so we can enjoy our quality of life and fulfill our life's purpose. To be influential in our families and communities, we must ensure we are cultured and that we value perspectives and knowledge that transcend our norms and comfort zones. Once black women improve upon our self-image, we can serve as influential leaders within our communities.

SECTION FIVE: CHALLENGE TO OUR QUEENS

- **A queen must be educated. Postsecondary schooling is highly encouraged and queens should make reading a daily habit.**
- **Be selfish when dating. Protect your feelings and set boundaries. Make a conscious decision to love**

yourself more. Love yourself as much as men love themselves.

- Understand and respect both phases of the vagina. In the first phase, enjoy sex with men who love and respect you and take advantage of the perks and leverage you possess during this phase! Preserve the phase two vagina for your husband and avoid bankrupting your vagina at all costs!!!
- To avoid controlling behavior or other forms of abuse from men, acquire financial stability for yourself.
- If you are a successful, wealthy woman, do not brag about your financial standing. Not only does this behavior emasculate good men, it will attract scammers and con artists who will try to take advantage of your resources.
- Make your health a priority in your life. Know your "numbers" (waist size, BMI and blood pressure) and take the appropriate measures to ensure that your numbers are in a healthy range.

- Understand the importance of healthy eating and make better dietary choices to lower your chances of acquiring preventable health issues. Stop eating fast food and processed foods and stop drinking soda. Limit your consumption of fried food, red meat and white/refined carbohydrates.
- Incorporate regular exercise into your routine. A 30 to 45 minute workout session, consisting of cardio and weight training, three to five times a week will suffice.
- Manage your mental health by eliminating controllable stressors from your life and utilize healthy ways of managing uncontrollable stressors such as cardio, meditation, yoga and therapy.
- A queen must be cultured. Travel is the best way to broaden your perspectives and expand your mind. Have a passport and make stepping out of your comfort zone and learning new ideas customary in your life experience.

CONCLUSION

"In every crisis there is a message. Crises are nature's way of forcing change—breaking down old structures, shaking loose negative habits so that something new and better can take their place." –Susan L. Taylor

There is no question that the state of Black America is still in disarray. We have yet to overcome the devastating psychological effects of slavery. It is certainly understandable that we are struggling with rebuilding, considering we are attempting to reverse the effects of the most dehumanizing debauchery ever imposed on any single demographic in this country. Additionally, we are attempting to find resolve in a country where our non-black neighbors are generally unsympathetic and often refuse to acknowledge the civil injustices placed upon us. Although the black experience in America has been outrageous and

CONCLUSION

unjust, we must continue taking the necessary steps toward making our communities reflective of greatness.

While on the path to rebuilding, we must confront one weakness that exists in the psyche of Black America. Many black people have developed a tendency to "allow life to happen to us" as opposed to directing our lives. We have adopted a sense of laziness and complacency which suggests that being reactive to life is acceptable. We must eliminate the "put it in God's hands" attitude when approaching situations we can in fact control or impact. When a person is not actively controlling or manipulating their surroundings to best serve their needs, their needs will not be met. In life we either work hard to enforce our own agenda or be subjected to someone else's. We are essentially "sitting ducks," reacting to the decisions others make, to achieve their agendas. It is time for black people to stop allowing life to happen to us. These passive and relaxed attitudes have stifled our growth. If our position in society has remained so irrelevant, police officers are aware they can publicly execute us without consequence, it is evident we are in need of reform.

CONCLUSION

Are we so far removed from the accomplishments we achieved during the Civil Rights Movement that we forgot why those initiatives were successful? We must adopt a unified mindset and develop our own trajectory for how we want to advance our communities. White America is not incentivized to create initiatives that advance the black community. We are responsible for our success. Black people must establish collective goals to advance our communities and be proactive in achieving them. We have to live with intention and purpose in the pursuit of our own goals. To achieve this, we must start by repairing our family structure. Strong families are the foundation for strong communities. Black women must initiate a movement to improve ourselves and our family structure, which will in turn rebuild the black community.

It is important to recognize the invaluable role black women play throughout this process. With this in mind, black women must regard themselves with the upmost importance and lead lives reflective of leaders, agents of change, and pillars in the community. We must give the appropriate attention and effort to improving all aspects of

CONCLUSION

our personal lives, so we may become worthy wives, mothers and astute leaders, capable of influencing positive change within the black community. We must ensure that we love ourselves enough and are demanding what we deserve from romantic relationships. We must try to better understand men and the role they play in our lives and communities. We must not overvalue or undervalue men and instead be demanding and set high standards so they will adequately protect and provide for us and our families. As queens, it is our responsibility to motivate and inspire black men to conduct themselves as kings. We must also be conscious of how we are treating other black women. We must come to terms with our insecurities and shortcomings and either eliminate them or accept them so we may carry ourselves like the "confident-woman" and always treat our fellow queens with love, appreciation and respect. We must reevaluate how we view motherhood. We must redefine "what is normal" and no longer deem it acceptable or respectable to bring life into this world without a loving, supportive husband, a safe and stable environment, adequate resources and a plan for success for our children's lives. It is unacceptable that 72 percent of black children are born

CONCLUSION

out of wedlock and raised in single parent households. As queens, it is our duty to drastically reduce this number and put an end to this epidemic. We must understand how raising children alone negatively impacts our lives, the lives of our children, our families and our communities. We must value our legacy and place adequate thought into building it, much like a queen would when constructing her kingdom. We must ensure that as queens, we are maintaining a positive lifestyle and self-image by investing in our happiness, our education, our health and in our cultural experiences. It is time for black women to initiate a movement of raised expectations and heightened standards for ourselves and our fellow queens. We must change many of our past habits and behaviors and instead strive for excellence. As a people, blacks have endured and overcome far too much to continue to allow mediocrity in our communities. It is disrespectful to our ancestors and counteractive to the strides they have made, to fail to live up to our full potential. It is time for black women to live with intention and purpose, making every decision with the goal of "Keeping Your Crown" in mind.

ABOUT THE AUTHORS

ABOUT THE AUTHORS

Joyce and Debra Glenn are identical twins and the youngest of four daughters in their large, close-knit family. Their father served in the U.S. Army for 25 years and as a result their family moved often due to their father's travel orders. They were stationed abroad in Germany and domestically in various states like Colorado, California and Georgia.

While growing up in the Glenn household, a heavy emphasis was placed on the importance of education. The twins both graduated from high school in the top tenth percentile of their graduating class and went on to graduate Magna Cum and Suma Cum Laude with Bachelor's Degrees in Accounting from Savannah State University. Joyce and Debra primarily funded their education with academic scholarships and are both members of the prestigious business honors society Beta Gamma Sigma. Aside from their academic pursuits, the twins got their start in the

ABOUT THE AUTHORS

entertainment industry as models at age 16. While living in California, the entertainment capital of the world, the twins were often approached with opportunities to model and act. At that time, the twins were extremely introverted and had little interest in the entertainment industry. Years later, while living in Atlanta, Georgia, the opportunity to pursue the entertainment industry was presented again. This time the twins acquiesced and began a modeling career while in high school. The twins' modeling assignments consisted of cosmetic contracts, hair ads, editorial spreads and catalogue work. Their appearances together in major music videos tremendously increased their popularity and inspired the twins to begin branding themselves as "The Glenn Twins." They had notable featured appearances in popular videos for major artists such as 50 Cent, Lil Wayne, Bow Wow, Jim Jones and R.Kelly. The twins eventually transitioned into acting and TV hosting as well. While working both together and individually, they landed roles in films, television and commercials. They had a major cameo in the feature film Fast And Furious 5 (Fast Five) and appeared in hit television shows such as The Rickey Smiley Show, Single Ladies and The Game.

ABOUT THE AUTHORS

Joyce and Debra admit that although they enjoy certain aspects of working in entertainment, their true passions lie with being business women and using their influence to ignite social change within the black community. The twins were raised by strong, intelligent and informed black parents from the south, who never neglected to share with the twins their heritage and the importance of advancing not only their own family, but also the state of Black America. The twins understand the importance of building strong black women and strong black families to create and sustain thriving black communities. *Keeping Your Crown* is the first of many pieces of literature Joyce and Debra will write to initiate the conversations needed to bring many black issues to light and encourage the change necessary to rebuild the black community.

Made in United States
North Haven, CT
15 March 2024